GameMaker Cookbook

Over 50 hands-on recipes to help you build exhilarating
games using the robust GameMaker system

Brandon Gardiner

BIRMINGHAM - MUMBAI

GameMaker Cookbook

First published: December 2015

Production reference: 1151215

Published by Packt Publishing Ltd.
Livery Place
35 Livery Street
Birmingham B3 2PB, UK.

ISBN 978-1-78439-984-9

www.packtpub.com

Credits

Author

Brandon Gardiner

Reviewers

Ryan Laley

John M. Walker, PE

Commissioning Editor

Nadeem N. Bagban

Acquisition Editor

Kirk D'costa

Content Development Editor

Siddhesh Salvi

Technical Editor

Madhunikita Sunil Chindarkar

Copy Editor

Rashmi Sawant

Project Coordinator

Nidhi Joshi

Proofreader

Safis Editing

Indexer

Hemangini Bari

Production Coordinator

Shantanu N. Zagade

Cover Work

Shantanu N. Zagade

About the Author

Brandon Gardiner is a game developer and designer living out his love of video games. Though he started his foray into games through 3D art and level design, he always kept a notebook of ideas for games and game mechanics he wished to see. When he discovered GameMaker: Studio, he found that he could bring these ideas to life.

He is a graduate of the first iteration of the game development program at Toronto's George Brown College. In college, he worked as an artist and designer on several game projects for outside companies, including tie-ins for children's television shows and educational titles. After graduating, he founded MechaBee Studios where, being the sole developer of mobile and PC games, he is a jack of all trades.

He also writes a blog at `http://www.gamemakerhq.com`, through which he hopes to build a resource for other independent developers. He lives with his wife in Toronto where he is a veteran of the annual Toronto Game Jam (`tojam.ca`), an active member of the International Game Developers Association.

About the Reviewers

Ryan Laley is an independent games designer. He has been a lecturer in video games design at South Essex College at further and higher education levels for over 5 years. He has been using GameMaker: Studio professionally during those years, and he continues to develop and publish games using it. He began his teaching career after graduating from university, and since then, he has covered every aspect of games development in his classes, including 2D and 3D.

In his spare time, he independently develops his own games and publishes them himself under the studio name of Friendly Fire games. His most recent projects focus on mobile phone platforms, with his latest release Blobb in 2015. His future projects will continue to expand on mobile platforms and eventually onto PCs.

I'd like to thank Jade for her continued support and allowing games to continue to be more than just a fun past-time, but a career as well.

John M. Walker, PE is a licensed professional engineer in industrial engineering and is currently a licensed full-time teacher in computer science and programing at Cleveland High School in Portland, Oregon. He has been teaching full time for the last 15 years for High School and Regional Professional Higher Ed conferences.

He has worked for more than 20 years as an information technology manager for high-technology firms dealing with systems administration and networking architecture and engineering. His favorite position was director of technology for the Portland Trail Blazers, while designing and constructing the Moda Center.

He has also reviewed *GameMaker Essentials*, *Packt Publishing*.

www.PacktPub.com

Support files, eBooks, discount offers, and more

For support files and downloads related to your book, please visit www.PacktPub.com.

Did you know that Packt offers eBook versions of every book published, with PDF and ePub files available? You can upgrade to the eBook version at www.PacktPub.com and as a print book customer, you are entitled to a discount on the eBook copy. Get in touch with us at service@packtpub.com for more details.

At www.PacktPub.com, you can also read a collection of free technical articles, sign up for a range of free newsletters and receive exclusive discounts and offers on Packt books and eBooks.

https://www2.packtpub.com/books/subscription/packtlib

Do you need instant solutions to your IT questions? PacktLib is Packt's online digital book library. Here, you can search, access, and read Packt's entire library of books.

Why Subscribe?

▶ Fully searchable across every book published by Packt

▶ Copy and paste, print, and bookmark content

▶ On demand and accessible via a web browser

Free Access for Packt account holders

If you have an account with Packt at www.PacktPub.com, you can use this to access PacktLib today and view 9 entirely free books. Simply use your login credentials for immediate access.

Table of Contents

Preface

Since 1999, GameMaker: Studio has enabled fledgling and experienced developers alike to help create video games quickly and easily. In the years since its initial release (as a program called Animo), GameMaker has grown and evolved into a viable commercial game engine that has helped developers release games for PC, Mac, mobile devices, and even the Microsoft Xbox and Sony PlayStation family of consoles.

During its progression, GameMaker has changed in many ways, adding new features and abilities to be taken advantage of by developers around the world. Though these features may be out of reach for new users, the goal of this book is to familiarize beginners and bring such elements within reach. This book is not just a how-to manual, it is an answer to the question "What can GameMaker do for me?"

By reading this book and completing the recipes therein, you will gain a greater understanding of GameMaker's capabilities as well as start them on the path to unlock their full potential.

What this book covers

Chapter 1, Game Plan – Creating Basic Gameplay, shows you how to create the basic elements of a game.

Chapter 2, It's Under Control – Exploring Various Control Schemes, helps you figure out how to implement user controls for a variety of devices.

Chapter 3, Let's Move It – Advanced Movement and Layout, teaches you more advanced ways to move players and non-player characters alike.

Chapter 4, Let's Get Physical – Using GameMaker's Physics System, introduces you to the physics system and demonstrates how GameMaker handles gravity, friction, and so on. You will also learn how to implement this system to make more realistic games.

Chapter 5, Now Hear This! – Music and Sound Effects, helps you pick up the ins and outs of GameMaker's audio system.

Chapter 6, It's All GUI! – Creating Graphical User Interface and Menus, discusses the most important element of the Graphical User Interface (GUI).

Chapter 7, Saving the Day – Saving Game Data, discusses how GameMaker handles how to save data as well as its various uses.

Chapter 8, Light 'em up! – Enhancing Your Game with Lighting Techniques, helps you understand how GameMaker's surfaces can add lighting effects to your game.

Chapter 9, Particle Man, Particle Man – Adding Polish to Your Game with Visual Effects and Particles, shows you how GameMaker handles particles and how you can draw players in with simple effects.

Chapter 10, Hello, World – Creating New Dimensions of Play Through Networking, teaches you how to create multiplayer games with GameMaker's networking capabilities.

What you need for this book

For this book, you will require the following software:

- ▶ Windows XP or above
- ▶ 512 MB RAM
- ▶ 128 MB graphics
- ▶ A screen resolution of 1024×600
- ▶ An Internet connection for some features

For a detailed platform-specific list of requirements, refer to http://www.yoyogames.com/studio/system-requirements.

Who this book is for

This book is intended for GameMaker: Studio enthusiasts who are looking to add more substance and improve their content. If you know your way around the program and have some basic GML skills but want to take them further, then this book is for you.

Sections

In this book, you will find several headings that appear frequently (Getting ready, How to do it, How it works, There's more, and See also).

To give clear instructions on how to complete a recipe, we use these sections as follows:

Getting ready

This section tells you what to expect in the recipe, and describes how to set up any software or any preliminary settings required for the recipe.

How to do it...

This section contains the steps required to follow the recipe.

How it works...

This section usually consists of a detailed explanation of what happened in the previous section.

There's more...

This section consists of additional information about the recipe in order to make the reader more knowledgeable about the recipe.

See also

This section provides helpful links to other useful information for the recipe.

Conventions

In this book, you will find a number of text styles that distinguish between different kinds of information. Here are some examples of these styles and an explanation of their meaning.

Code words in text, database table names, folder names, filenames, file extensions, pathnames, dummy URLs, user input, and Twitter handles are shown as follows: "Create a sprite and name it `spr_enemy_patrol`."

A block of code is set as follows:

```
x1: -16
y1: -24
x2: 16
y2: -34
back color: black
bar color: green to red
```

New terms and **important words** are shown in bold. Words that you see on the screen, for example, in menus or dialog boxes, appear in the text like this: "Click **Add Event**, then **Other**, and select **Animation End**."

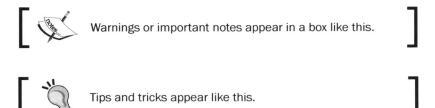

Warnings or important notes appear in a box like this.

Tips and tricks appear like this.

Reader feedback

Feedback from our readers is always welcome. Let us know what you think about this book—what you liked or disliked. Reader feedback is important for us as it helps us develop titles that you will really get the most out of.

To send us general feedback, simply e-mail feedback@packtpub.com, and mention the book's title in the subject of your message.

If there is a topic that you have expertise in and you are interested in either writing or contributing to a book, see our author guide at www.packtpub.com/authors.

Customer support

Now that you are the proud owner of a Packt book, we have a number of things to help you to get the most from your purchase.

Downloading the example code

You can download the example code files from your account at http://www.packtpub.com for all the Packt Publishing books you have purchased. If you purchased this book elsewhere, you can visit http://www.packtpub.com/support and register to have the files e-mailed directly to you.

Downloading the color images of this book

We also provide you with a PDF file that has color images of the screenshots/diagrams used in this book. The color images will help you better understand the changes in the output. You can download this file from https://www.packtpub.com/sites/default/files/downloads/9849OS_ColorImages.pdf.

Errata

Although we have taken every care to ensure the accuracy of our content, mistakes do happen. If you find a mistake in one of our books—maybe a mistake in the text or the code—we would be grateful if you could report this to us. By doing so, you can save other readers from frustration and help us improve subsequent versions of this book. If you find any errata, please report them by visiting http://www.packtpub.com/submit-errata, selecting your book, clicking on the **Errata Submission Form** link, and entering the details of your errata. Once your errata are verified, your submission will be accepted and the errata will be uploaded to our website or added to any list of existing errata under the Errata section of that title.

To view the previously submitted errata, go to https://www.packtpub.com/books/content/support and enter the name of the book in the search field. The required information will appear under the **Errata** section.

Piracy

Piracy of copyrighted material on the Internet is an ongoing problem across all media. At Packt, we take the protection of our copyright and licenses very seriously. If you come across any illegal copies of our works in any form on the Internet, please provide us with the location address or website name immediately so that we can pursue a remedy.

Please contact us at copyright@packtpub.com with a link to the suspected pirated material.

We appreciate your help in protecting our authors and our ability to bring you valuable content.

Questions

If you have a problem with any aspect of this book, you can contact us at questions@packtpub.com, and we will do our best to address the problem.

1
Game Plan – Creating Basic Gameplay

In this chapter, we'll cover the following:

- ▶ Animating a sprite
- ▶ Moving your player
- ▶ Adding projectiles
- ▶ Creating hazards
- ▶ Programming basic enemies
- ▶ Setting up player health and lives
- ▶ Creating a scoring mechanism
- ▶ Creating win/lose scenarios

Introduction

GameMaker is a great tool for people interested in various aspects of game development. It can be used to quickly create simple, playable games, or even churn out hits like *Hotline Miami* and *Gunpoint*. Want to take part in a game jam? GameMaker can save you hours of coding, and as many headaches. Have a game mechanic you want to visualize? GameMaker is great for prototyping; it can do that. Well, *you* will have to do the work. GameMaker will just make it *faster* and *easier*.

Let's take a look at just how quickly and easily we can make a game using GameMaker's *drag-and-drop* interface.

Animating a sprite

Animated sprites can be made by importing frames from a sprite sheet or by creating individual images in a 3rd party program. What happens, though, if you don't have access to these methods? GameMaker includes its own image editor that, while not as versatile as programs like Photoshop, has received some recent upgrades that can help you create some decent animations.

Getting ready

Let's make a player character sprite with a simple walk cycle. If you haven't already, now would be a good time to open GameMaker, start a new project, and create a sprite. Name the sprite `spr_player_walk`.

 Using descriptive names like this allows you to categorize your assets, which makes finding the right asset much easier.

How to do it...

As mentioned before, you can use 3rd party art programs to create your own sprites and import them to GameMaker. If you're more interested in just making something that moves, I've included the files necessary to create an animated sprite; simply load them from sprite properties and you're almost good to go.

With that out of the way, let's look at using GameMaker's built-in Sprite Editor.

1. With **Sprite Properties** open, click on **Edit Sprite** to open the Sprite Editor.

2. Click the **Create a New Sprite** button near the top left; the icon looks like a blank document. The default size for a sprite is 32×32 (pixels) but let's change that to 64×64.

3. Click on **Animation** and select **Set Length** from the menu. Set this animation to 12 frames. You should now have 12 blank images beginning with `image 0` and ending with `image 11`. The numbering system here is important when it comes to coding, so keep that in mind.

4. If you double-click on the first image the Image Editor will open; this is where you'll draw and edit your frames, thus animating the sprite. At first glance, the editor is reminiscent of simple bitmap editors that allow you to paint images using your mouse or tablet. If you open the **Image** menu, however, you'll find that you have access to more advanced options such as edge smoothing, alpha and opacity controls, and even shadows.

5. If you open the **View** menu, you'll find you can toggle the visibility of a grid over the image. Each space in this grid represents one pixel in the image, making this tool perfect for creating pixel art in GameMaker. Using this and other tools available, here's the first frame I made for our character:

The Image Editor comes with another feature that is great for animating your sprites: **Onion Skin**. **Onion Skin** allows you to, while working on one frame of an animation, view the following and preceding frames. You can set how many frames you want visible, both backwards and forwards, and use the **Onion Skin** value to change the opacity of those frames to alter their visibility while working. This can help you paint each form and make the animation more fluid because you can see where you've been and where you're going. A useful addition to this is the **Scratch Page**. Simply hit the *J* key to be taken to and from a frame that doesn't actually exist in your animation, but allows you to cut and paste image elements. It's a big help when you want to move separate pieces of an image from one frame to another.

The **Scratch Page** looks the same as the standard **Image Editor** window and holds whatever you paste in it.

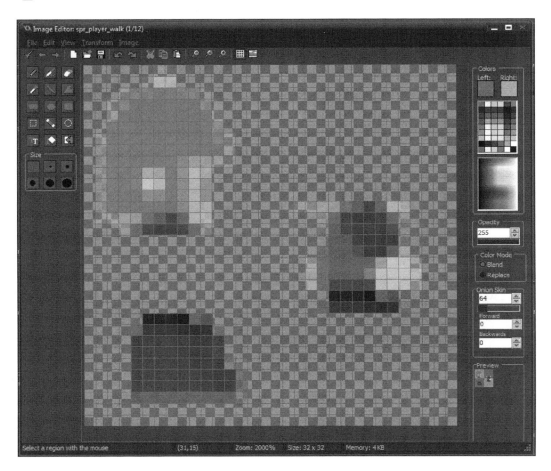

There you have it; you've animated a sprite for use in a game. That's a great first step, but we're not finished. If you use this sprite on your character it will appear as though he's walking at all times. I don't know about you, but that's not what I want to see in a game. You could animate an idle sprite, which is ideal for a polished look, but we're going to speed this up by using a single-frame idle pose.

1. Open up **Sprite Properties** for spr_player_walk and click **Edit Sprite**.
2. Select whichever frame you feel looks best as an idle pose (I chose the first frame).

3. Click **Edit**, then click **Copy**.
4. Close **Sprite Properties**, create a new sprite, and call it `spr_player_idle`.
5. Click **Edit Sprite**, press *Ctrl + V* on your keyboard to paste the copied frame, and close the editor and **Sprite Properties** window.

Done. You now have a second sprite for a single character.

How it works...

As we've just seen, it's possible to create fully animated characters without the use of a 3rd party program. While other programs give you many more options not found in GameMaker, such as layers, you still have access to the fundamentals you need to get the job done. The editor is great for pixel art and **Onion Skin** makes animating *a lot* smoother by showing you adjacent frames.

There's more...

Now, we've only made sprites for two states of our character's being: idle and walking right. There are many other sprites you may want to consider if you're looking to build a full game. Think about other games you've played; how many different movements and poses do they incorporate? Walking, running, jumping, rolling, punching, shooting, and so on, you get the idea. When designing a game, any actions you intend for your player character should be listed and planned out because you need to consider just how many sprites you'll need. Will they be animated? Will they look different depending on what direction the player is facing, or can they be mirrored? How long will it take for the animation to play out? These are all important questions, but they get easier to answer with each game you make.

See also

Sprites used for GUI will be discussed in *Chapter 6, It's All GUI! – Creating Graphical User Interface and Menus*, while sprite-based VFX are used in *Chapter 9, Particle Man, Particle Man – Adding Polish to Your Game with Visual Effects and Particles*.

Moving your player

There are many different types of games with different visuals and play styles. Some games are devoid of a visible player character but most, especially 2D games, have the player controlling a sprite or 3D model onscreen. We're going to take a quick look at putting a character in front of the player that he/she can control.

Getting ready

You've animated some sprites, but animated sprites won't do you any good without a character to which they can be applied. Create a new object and call it `obj_player`. Under **Sprite**, click the **menu icon** and select `spr_player_idle`.

How to do it...

1. In `obj_player`'s **Object Properties** window, click **Add Event**, then click **Keyboard** and select `<Right>` from the menu. This event will allow you to make things happen while you're pressing the right arrow key on your keyboard. What we want to have happen is for our player character to move to the right and to have his right facing walk cycle play while he is doing it, so let's do it.

2. Under the **Main1** tab on the right side of the **Object Properties** window, drag **Change Sprite** (it looks like a green *Pac-Man*) and drop it in the **Actions** box.

3. The actions we want apply to `obj_player`, so select **Applies** to **Self**.

4. Since we want to use `spr_player_walk` in this case, select the sprite from the drop-down menu.

5. `Subimage` defaults to `0`, but this tells GameMaker that we only want to show the first frame of the animation. Since we want to have the entire animation play, you'll need to set this value to `-1`, which tells GameMaker to ignore the subimage count.

6. The sprite's play speed can be altered by setting the **Speed** option to a value between `0` and `1`. Set the value to `0.8` so that the walk cycle will play at 80 percent of the room's frame rate and close this box.

    We want the player character to move right when the right arrow key is pressed but we don't want him to simply walk right off the screen. How mad would you be if the character you were controlling simply gave up, said *That's it, I'm out of here!* and disappeared off screen? Sounds like an entirely frustrating experience. Since we don't want this to happen, let's make sure it can't. For that, you'll need to add a variable check before your character goes anywhere.

7. Under the **Control** tab, drag and drop **Test Variable** to the **Actions** box.

8. We want to test the variable `x`, which is the player's x coordinate or horizontal position. Since we want to the player to stay on-screen, we'll set the `value` to `room_width-16` and the `operation` will be `less than`.

9. Close the **Test Variable** box and under the **Move** tab, drag and drop **Jump to Position** to the **Actions** box.

10. Set `x` to `4`, leave `y` as `0`, and make sure `Relative` is checked. If you were to test this out now, your player will begin moving to the right as his walk cycle animation played. The problem is that now it doesn't stop.

11. Add another event but this time choose **Key Release <Right>**. Add **Change Sprite** to the **Actions** box but this time select `spr_player_idle` from the menu. This time, if you were to run a test, your player would walk right when holding the right arrow key and go back to his idle pose when it is released.

    These same steps can be repeated for all directions using corresponding keyboard events but you need to take into consideration whether or not you need to mirror the sprites. If you've created separate sprites for each direction you'll simply choose which sprite you'll need at the time. If, however, you've opted to mirror the sprites, you'll need to add one more thing to each key event.

12. Under the **Main1** tab, drag and drop **Transform Sprite** into the Actions box for each key event (key release events included) and modify the `xscale` (for horizontal mirroring) or the `yscale` (for vertical flipping). Setting the value to -1 would flip the image and setting it to 1 would revert it to its original facing. If the image is already facing that way, no change is made. Avoid using the options in the `Mirror` menu, as these selections alter the image from its present state instead of assigning a value. This would mean that if you hit the left arrow key, and the character was already facing left, he would flip and face right. That would be confusing!

This and any other drag and drop function in GameMaker can also be used in code and scripts. In fact, coding them yourself often allows for greater control over how they work.

How it works...

The movement discussed in this section is quite simple. In this case, you've instructed GameMaker to make your character move left or right and play the walk animation (facing the proper direction) as he goes. Using jump to position allows you to move a character to any point in the screen or, as you did here, move the character relative to its current position, adding the entered values to existing coordinates. Using a negative value would subtract from the current coordinates, causing the character to move in the opposite direction. If you want your character to move up or down you would change the value of y and leave x as 0. I encourage you to play around with the values entered, as this will change the player's speed.

There's more...

It might seem like this section had a lot of text to set up very simple movement, but I can assure you it is all necessary. This section and the rest of the chapter set up some core ideas that will recur throughout your GameMaker experience and will be explored much further later on.

See also

Several methods of advanced player movement and controls will be demonstrated in *Chapter 2, It's Under Control – Exploring Various Control Schemes*, and *Chapter 3, Let's Move It – Advanced Movement and Layout*.

Adding projectiles

Now that our character can move, logically (or rather, illogically), we want to give him a gun. Though countless games offer projectiles as part of the gameplay, there are a great number of design choices to consider that will ultimately alter the way the player plays. We're going to create simple projectiles right now but later in the book we'll discuss different design choices for creating and controlling gameplay.

Getting ready

1. Create a sprite, call it `spr_projectile`, and load the images you would like to use; you can use a single, static image, but it looks much better if your projectile has a brief animation. (I've provided a projectile animation in the downloaded project files. The sprite is 16px by 16px.)

2. Now create an object for the projectile (`obj_projectile`) and assign the sprite you made.

We want to create a projectile at our character's location whenever the player hits the Spacebar. On creation of the projectile, we want GameMaker to verify the direction the player is facing and send it flying in that direction. Before GameMaker can check the direction, though, we need to create a variable that *tells* GameMaker which direction the object is actually facing. It sounds convoluted but in execution it's really fairly simple, so let's begin.

How to do it...

1. Open the **Object Properties** for `obj_player` and add a **Create** event.
2. Under the **Control** tab, drag and drop **Set Variable** to the **Actions** box.
3. Name the variable `dir` and set the value to `1`.
4. In the `Keyboard` event for `right`, drag and drop Set Variable from the Control tab and have it set `dir` to `1`.
5. Do the same for the left keyboard event but have it set `dir` to `-1`.
6. Now create a **Key Press** event and select `<Space>`.
7. Under the Main1 tab, drag and drop **Create** instance to the **Actions** box.
8. Select `obj_projectile` from the menu but leave the x and y values as 0.

9. Open the **Object Properties** for `obj_projectile` and add a **Create** event.

10. Under the **Control** tab, drag and drop **Test Variable** to the **Actions** box.

11. Under `Applies to` select `obj_player` and have it test whether or not the variable `dir` is equal to a value of `1`.

12. Now, under the **Move** tab, drag and drop **Move Fixed** to the **Actions** box and have our projectile move to the right at a speed of `8`.

13. In the same **Create** event, repeat these steps but check `dir` for a value of `-1` and have the projectile move to the left. The `obj_projectile` properties window should look like this:

There's one last thing we should look at, here, and that's how *often* our player character can shoot. As it is right now he can shoot every time the Spacebar is pressed. Imagine our character is holding a handgun. Now think about how quickly the player could potentially press the Spacebar, over and over. I don't know about you but I imagine a handgun that can shoot *that* fast must be magical; maybe a wizard made it. There is a way around this magical handgun made by wizards, and that way involves **alarms** and **variables**.

1. Open up the properties for `obj_player` once more and, in the **Create** event, drag and drop another **Set Variable** to the **Actions** box.

2. Call the variable `shoot` and set the value to `1`.

3. In the `Key Press` event for `Space`, drag **Set Variable** to the **Actions** box and set `shoot` to `0`.

4. Under the **Main2** tab, drag **Set Alarm** to the **Actions** box and set `Alarm 0` to `30`.

5. Now click on **Add Event**, select **Alarm 0**, and drag **Set Variable** to the **Actions** box and have it set `shoot` back to 1.

6. There's just one final change to make, now. Go back to the **Space** key press event and drag **Test Variable** to the **Actions** box and have it test if `shoot` is equal to 1.

7. Make sure this is the first thing GameMaker does when Spacebar is pressed by dragging it to the top of the list.

8. Now, the rest of the actions here should only be carried out if `shoot` is equal to 1. To make sure this is the case, drag **Start Block** from the **Control** tab and drop it above **Create Instance**, and drag **End Block** to the bottom of the list. The Spacebar key press event should now look like this:

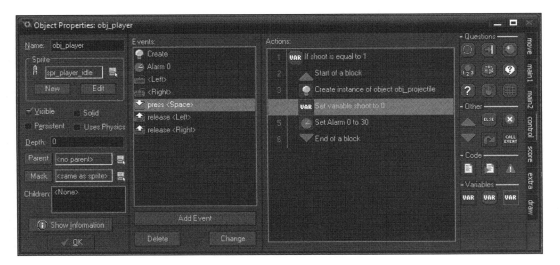

Congratulations! You now have a player that can shoot projectiles in the direction he is facing and do so at a realistic rate. This outcome is *much* more appealing than having a player who fires his gun wherever he pleases at incredible rates. You're a loose cannon, player!

How it works...

In order to make your character shoot projectiles, we've had to use several important elements of programming with GameMaker, namely variables and alarms. When the Spacebar is hit, GameMaker first has to check whether or not the variable `shoot` is equal to 1. If not, nothing happens. You could hit the spacebar as many times as you want, but unless `shoot` equals 1, you'll get nothing out of it. Now, assuming `shoot` *does* equal 1, GameMaker moves on to create a projectile in the same place as the player, which is (0, 0) *relative* to wherever the player object is sitting. If you want the projectile to be created *near* the player, say to give the appearance that the projectile is coming out of a gun, you could change the coordinate values for (x, y).

At the same time, GameMaker is setting `shoot` to `0` to prevent the player from shooting again right away, and setting an alarm to 30 steps. At the end of those 30 steps, `shoot` is set back to `1`. Each step is the same as one frame in-game, meaning if the game is running at 60 frames per second, the player can fire every half-second.

Once the projectile is created, GameMaker is testing another variable we set: `dir`. This is simply to tell GameMaker in which direction the player is facing and GameMaker then sends the projectile off in that direction. Bam. Projectiles. No pun intended.

See also

Projectiles will be expanded on in *Chapter 9, Particle Man, Particle Man – Adding Polish to Your Game with Visual Effects and Particles*.

Creating hazards

So our player can move and shoot. That's great, but what fun is that when there are no obstacles? Hazards offer a great challenge and can even be the core of your gameplay. How boring would *Mario Kart* be without banana peels? Or *Pitfall* without...well, the pits? Video game hazards come in many forms and, if you play games, you've likely encountered most, if not all of them. Spikes, lasers, electrical traps, and falling objects are a few examples, but they have at least one thing in common: if your player character touches them, he/she will be hurt or killed. Now, in most games the latter isn't permanent, what with health bars and lives (we'll get into those later), but it remains a major part of the gameplay. Let's look at creating some simple hazards that can give your players a hard time.

Getting ready

In-game hazards can come in many forms and various visual styles. Like the projectiles we discussed previously they can be static images, but they look much better as animated sprites. We're going to build a spike trap; you can use your own art, but I've included an animated sprite in the downloadable files.

1. Create a sprite, name it `spr_hazard_spike`, and load the necessary images. Before we move, on you're going to need to set up the sprite's collision mask. Sprites are assigned a collision mask by default but you can modify it to your own needs. We only want the trap to be activated and for the player to take damage when the spikes are actually touched, as opposed to the area around the trap.

2. Under **Collision Checking** make sure **Precise collision checking** is selected.

3. Click **Modify Mask** and, under **Shape**, select **Precise**. To the left of that is a slider that allows you to specify **Alpha Tolerance**. This is useful because it allows you to shrink and grow the mask according to the sprite's outline (the empty space around it being an alpha map).

Once you save your selections we're ready to get started.

How to do it...

1. Begin by creating a new object called `obj_hazard_spike` and assigning the sprite you made previously.

2. Add a **Create** event and drag and drop two instances of **Set Variable**. One will set `image_speed` to 0, the other will set `trap_set` to 1.

3. Add a **Collision** event with `obj_player` as the target.

4. Drag and drop **Test Variable** to the **Actions** box, checking that `trap_set` is equal to 1.

5. Place both a **Start** and **End Block** in the **Actions** box. Within this block you'll need two **Set Variables**; one that sets `trap_set` to 0, and another that sets `image_speed` to 1.

6. Still within the block, set `Alarm 0` to 60. Your **Actions** box should now look like this:

>
> **Downloading the example code**
> You can download the example code files from your account at `http://www.packtpub.com` for all the Packt Publishing books you have purchased. If you purchased this book elsewhere, you can visit `http://www.packtpub.com/support` and register to have the files e-mailed directly to you.

7. Create the event for `Alarm 0`.

8. In the **Actions** box, drag and drop **Set Variable**, setting `image_speed` to 1.

9. Drag and drop **Set Alarm**, setting `Alarm 1` to `30`.

10. Add the event for `Alarm 1`, where you'll drag `Set Variable` and have it set `trap_set` to `1`.

11. Add a **Step Event** and drag **Test Variable** to the **Actions** box and have it test whether or not `image_index` is equal to `4`.

12. This should be followed by a **Start** and **End Block**. Within this block should be a **Test Variable** that checks whether or not `alarm[0]` is *greater* than `0`, as well as *another* **Start** and **End Block**.

13. Within *this* block you'll need a **Set Variable** that sets `image_speed` to `0`. When you're done, the **Actions** box should look like this:

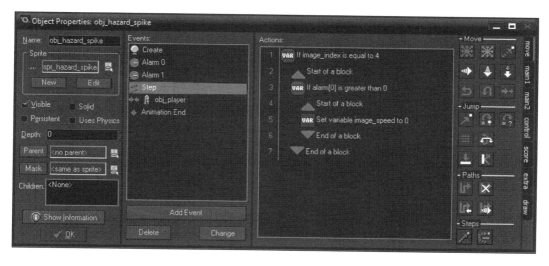

14. Finally, click **Add Event**, then **Other**, and select **Animation End**.

15. All you need in the **Actions** box here is a **Set Variable** that sets `image_speed` to `0`.

Got all that? It's a lot to do all at once, but we'll go through what it does, step by step. The good news is that you now have a spike trap that springs when touched by the player and stays sprung for a bit before retracting. There's a good reason behind this that we'll explore a little further once we get into player health.

How it works...

The trap you've just made uses collision detection and alarms to set and reset variables that control the trap's state. On creation, GameMaker sets the `image_speed` to 0, keeping the animation on the 1st frame, and establishes the variable `trap_set`, which will only be used by this particular instance of the spike trap. Think of `trap_set` as a sort of on/off switch, using binary (0 or 1) to dictate its current state. When the player collides with the trap, GameMaker checks whether or not the trap is *on*. If `trap_set` is equal to 1 (on), GameMaker proceeds to set `image_speed` to 1 (so the animation will begin to play), set `Alarm` 0 to 60 steps, and reset `trap_set` to 0 so that the spike trap will not be activated over and over again. This is to give the player a chance to move away from the trap to avoid being injured a second time. The **Step Event** checks every single step to see whether or not the sprite's animation has advanced to frame number 4. If it has, it then checks whether or not `Alarm` 0 is still counting down. If it is, `image_speed` is set to 0, so that the animation remains on the 4th frame (in the *up* position) until `Alarm` 0 is finished counting down. When it has, the `image_speed` is set back to 1, allowing the animation to continue, and `Alarm` 1 is set to 30 steps. The animation can continue (retracting the spikes) but once it reaches the last frame, the **Animation End** event then sets `image_speed` to 0 again, preventing the animation from looping. The last thing to happen in this long list of events is the end of `Alarm` 1, which simply gives `trap_set` a value of 1, thereby *resetting* the trap to be used again.

It's a lot to take in at once, but creating this trap is a great demonstration of the programming logic we're going to get into later on. For now, enjoy your new spike trap!

Programming basic enemies

Enemies are more or less an extension of hazards; the basic idea is that if they touch (or shoot a projectile that touches) the player, the player is injured or killed. Only in games, though, not in real life. There is one difference here: enemies move. You can create enemies that will march to their deaths (think *Goombas* in the *Mario Bros* games), patrol a given area (think soldiers in the *Metal Gear* games), or even actively hunt the player (think ghosts in *Pac-Man*). For now, we're going to take a look at a simple enemy that will patrol a straight line.

Getting ready

As with everything we've done so far in this chapter, you'll need sprites to represent your enemy. You can make your own or you can use the one included in the downloaded files. It's acceptable to use the same sprite for different types of enemies but, from a game design perspective, it's a good idea to differentiate. This will make it easier for your player to identify the enemy types and react accordingly.

Create a sprite and name it `spr_enemy_patrol`. Load the associated images from the files provided, or create your own, and be sure to set up the collision mask.

How to do it...

1. Create an object called `obj_enemy_patrol` and assign the sprite you just made.

2. Add a **Create** event and drag and drop **Set Variable** that sets `image_speed` to `0.6`.

3. Drag and drop **Set Variable**, which will set `dir` as `-1`, and **Transform Sprite**, which will change the `xscale` to `-1`. Now, that's the simple part. The rest of the actions for (for the moment) will be handled by a **Step** event.

4. Add a **Step** event. This is where you'll need to run several tests in order to dictate your enemy's movement.

5. Drag and drop **Test Variable** and have it check whether or not `dir` is equal to `-1`.

6. Beneath this, drag a **Start** and **End Block**, within which you'll add a **Test Variable** that checks whether or not `x` is greater than `16`.

7. Below this, you'll need a **Start** and **End Block**, between which you should place **Moved Fixed**, and set it to move `left` at a speed of `1`.

8. Under all of the preceding boxes, drag and drop another **Start** and **End Block**.

9. Within this block, place a **Test Variable** that checks whether `x` is less than or equal to `16`, followed by another **Start** and **End Block**.

10. Within *this* block you will need a **Set Variable** that sets `dir` to `1`, a **Transform Sprite** that changes `xscale` to `1`, and a **Move Fixed** that sets the move direction to the `right` at a speed of `1`.

You now have exactly *half* of the actions required for a patrolling enemy. At this point you can do one of two things: You could copy this entire set of actions, paste the copies directly below the existing actions, and go about changing the variables to their exact opposites, or you could drag and drop new blocks in the same order, but set the variables to their opposites. The former is much faster, but the latter will help you learn more about programming logic. In any respect, your **Actions** box should look like this:

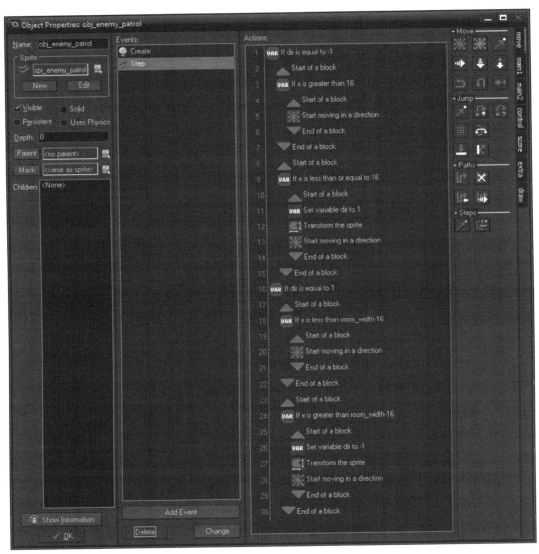

How it works...

While this **Step** event contains a lot of actions, it is really doing something quite simple. GameMaker is checking, every game step, for the patrolling enemy's state and position. If headed left and his position on the room's x coordinate is more than 16, he'll continue on in that direction. Once he gets past this point, GameMaker switches his direction, flips the sprite and sends him off to the other side of the room until his x coordinate reaches the room width minus 16 pixels, rinse and repeat.

There's more...

This method of creating a patrolling enemy is a simple enough way to move your enemy in a set space. I chose to have him walk right across the entire room, but you could also have him walk within a smaller space. Another way to accomplish this is to create left and right boxes, remove their visibility by unchecking the `Visible` box in **Object Properties**, and placing them at either end of the area you want patrolled. In the enemy's properties, instead of having everything in the **Step** event, you can control when they change direction by when they collide with the invisible boxes. The same actions would apply; they would just be executed in a different way. This just goes to show you that there are many possible solutions to all of the problems you may encounter when making games; you just have to find them.

See also

Paths will be discussed in *Chapter 4, Let's Get Physical – Using GameMaker's Physics System*.

Setting up player health and lives

Any action game involving a player controlled character is likely to have some sort of "health" and "life" system. These are terms long used in video games that are used in conjunction with how your character is abstractly "alive" within the game itself. In reality, health and life in games are simply numbers whereby you lose a chance to play or even the game itself when they reach zero. GameMaker makes keeping track of these numbers quite easy when it comes to the drag and drop actions, so we're going to look at how we can add these elements to our player character.

Getting ready

Since this recipe involves making additions to your existing player character, you don't need to do much. You'll need a sprite to indicate your player's lives (call it `spr_life`) but other than that all you need to do now is open the `obj_player` **Object Properties** window.

How to do it...

1. In the **Create** event, from the **Score** tab, drag and drop the **Set Health** action into the **Actions** box and set `Health` to `100`.

2. From the same tab, drag and drop **Set Lives** and set it to `3`.

3. Add a **Set Variable** to the **Actions** box and set `hit` to `0`.

4. Click **Add Event**, then **Collision**, and select `obj_enemy_patrol` from the menu.

5. Add **Test Variable** to the **Actions** box and have it check for whether `hit` equals `0`.

6. Below, drag and drop **Start** and **End Block**, and within that block add **Set Health** with a relative value of `-20`.

7. Add **Set Variable**, setting `hit` to `1`.

8. Add Set `Alarm 1` and set it to `60` steps. Repeat these actions using `obj_hazard_spike` in place of your enemy.

9. Add an event for **Alarm 1** and drag **Set Variable** to the **Actions** box, setting hit to `0`.

10. Add the event **Draw GUI** and, from the score tab, drag **Draw Health** to the **Actions** box.

11. Make sure **Relative** is checked and, under the appropriate headings, enter the following values:

    ```
    x1: -16
    y1: -24
    x2: 16
    y2: -34
    back color: black
    bar color: green to red
    ```

12. Drag and drop **Draw Life Images** to the **Actions** box and enter the following values:

    ```
    x: room_width-64
    y: 64
    image: spr_life
    ```

13. Create a **Step** event and add a **Test Variable** that checks if `health` is equal to `0`.

14. Below that, drag a **Start** and **End Block** and within that block add **Set Variable** `lives` to `-1` relative, and **Set Variable** `health` to `100`.

How it works...

Health and lives are very straightforward, with GameMaker doing a lot of the work for you when using the drag and drop actions. Essentially, GameMaker has created the variable `health` and you've set it to a value of `100`. You've also created the variable `hit`, which you use to control when you can be injured. If `hit` is set to `0` (off) then you can be hit by an enemy or hazard. If you *are* hit by one of them you lose 20 health points and the variable `hit` is set to `1`. This is to prevent contact with an enemy continuously draining your health, as it is being checked every step. An alarm is set to 60 steps and at the end of that countdown `hit` is set back to `0`, meaning you can be injured once more.

The **Step** event is also constantly checking for when your health reaches `0`. When it does, the `lives` variable is decreased by `1` and your health is reset to `100`.

There's more...

In this case we set the health bar to a specific coordinate relative to the player's position. This was purely a design choice to show you that you have options. You can set the health bar to a static position on the screen, much like we did for the lives indicator. As for the lives indicator, using the **Draw Lives** action instead of **Draw Life Images** allows you to indicate the player's remaining lives with text and numbers.

Creating scoring mechanism

In the days of arcades, a high score was king. It wasn't enough to beat a game; you had to get in the top 10 highest scores in order to claim local fame. Once your score was high enough to knock someone out of the top ten, the victory could be finalized by putting your initials next to it. Or a dirty word. Not that I've ever done that....

Regardless, a lot of games today don't rely on a scoring system, but focus on the story, experience, or multiplayer rankings. Let's bring back a little piece of gaming history by creating a simple scoring mechanism.

Getting ready

This recipe does not involve any new sprites or other assets but does require a new object. Call the object `obj_score` and leave the sprite box blank.

How to do it...

1. In the **Object Properties** for obj_score, add a **Create** event.

2. Drag **Set Score** from the **Score** tab to the **Actions** box, and have it set the score to 0.

3. Create a **Draw GUI** event and drag **Draw Score** to the **Actions** tab with the following values:

   ```
   x: 32
   y: 32
   caption: Score:
   ```

4. Close the obj_score **Object Properties** window and open obj_enemy_patrol.

5. Add a **Collision** event with obj_projectile and, from the **Main1** tab, drag and drop **Destroy Instance** to the **Actions** box (Applies to: self).

6. Drag **Set Score** to the **Actions** box and change the new score to 10 relative.

7. Close the **Object Properties** window and open obj_projectile.

8. Add a **Collision** event with obj_enemy_patrol and drag and drop **Destroy** instance at **Position** like you did previously.

How it works...

GameMaker is again doing a lot of the heavy lifting, here. You created obj_score to keep track of scoring. Not assigning a sprite to it will allow the object to be in a room, affecting the game, without being seen. The rest of the recipe is simply placing the score counter as a GUI element, checking for collisions between projectile and enemy, and adding points and destroying the two when they collide.

There's more...

In this recipe, obj_score acted as what's referred to as a controller object. These objects are often invisible and control specific aspects of the game. Since an object needs to be active in order for its actions and variables to be used, any aspect of the game that needs to be present without interruption should be assigned to a controller. I use controllers for music, HUD, global variables, and more.

See also

Most chapters going forward will deal with controllers and their various functions.

Creating win/lose scenarios

The term "game" has many different definitions, to the point where experts can't always agree what makes a game. Most definitions, though, determine that games are only such if they involve both win and lose scenarios. I mean, who wants to play a game you can't win or lose?

Getting ready

This recipe, again, does not necessitate new sprites or even objects. We'll be relying on existing objects but we'll be adding some new variables. Start by opening the **Object Properties** for obj_player.

How to do it...

1. In the **Step** event you should already have the actions that check the value of health. Beneath all of that, drag and drop **Test Variable** and have it check whether lives equals 0.

2. Below that, from the **Main2** tab, drag **Restart Game** to the **Actions** tab.

3. Close obj_player and open obj_score.

4. Create a **Step** event and drag **Test Variable** to the **Actions** box and have it check whether score is equal to 100.

5. Below that, drag **Restart Game** from the **Main2** tab.

How it works...

As you may have guessed by the names of the actions, you are simply asking GameMaker to check the values of score and lives, and restarting the game when they reach a certain point. In previous recipes you set the score to increase by 10 whenever you shot an enemy. If you shoot 10 enemies, the game will restart. You set the lives variable to 3 but had it decrease by 1 every time your health reached 0. Once you have no lives left, the game restarts.

There's more...

Using Game Restart in this scenario is arbitrary; it is simply there to demonstrate that you can tell GameMaker to change the game's state based on your score, health, or number of lives. Under the **Main1** tab in **Object Properties** you can find actions that take you to other rooms you may have created. This can be used to go from one level to another.

See also

The *Chapter 6, It's All GUI! – Creating Graphical User Interface and Menus*, deals with more advanced GUI and *Chapter 7, Saving the Day – Saving Game Data*, covers save systems and leaderboards.

2
It's Under Control – Exploring Various Control Schemes

In this recipe, we'll cover the following topics:

- Listing controls
- Creating 2D movement
- Adding a **Run** button
- Making your character jump
- Using a point-and-click interface
- Following the cursor
- Setting up a controller
- Utilizing analogue joystick acceleration
- Adding tap control
- Using swipes
- Moving characters or objects by tilting a device

Introduction

If someone gives you a videogame controller and asks you to play the game, your first question would likely be "How do I play?" This is a simple way of asking "How do I control what I see on the screen?" A game's *controls* are a major part of the gameplay as your player's input essentially determines everything. An otherwise good game can be rendered unplayable by an awkward or overly complicated control scheme. This is compounded by the push toward touch controls that, especially in the mobile game market, demand a simple interface with a lot of developers opting for a one-touch gameplay.

Just because game controls are trending toward simplistic, it doesn't mean you need to shoehorn your game to work in this fashion. The most important thing about your control setup is that it needs to fit to your game's style. You won't see one-touch controls on a first-person shooter just like you won't see a memory game that requires two joysticks and eight buttons; it just doesn't make sense. For this reason, we're going to take a look at several control options, including touch controls, in order to give you the tools you need to make a game that *feels* right.

Let's take a quick look at the controls we have at our disposal.

Keyboard controls

Do you have a computer? If so, there are chances that you have a keyboard to go with it. Let's put it to work with some simple movement code by:

- Creating 2D movement
- Adding a **Run** button
- Making your character jump

Mouse controls

Your mouse is an incredibly versatile peripheral utilized by almost every modern program. If you've ever played a game on your computer, it's almost guaranteed that you've used your mouse at least for one. We'll look at how we can implement mouse controls for gameplay with:

- Using a point-and-click interface
- Following the cursor

Gamepad controls

PC games have been using gamepad controls for years. Today, gamepads are supported by many other operating systems, including Android, iOS, and even HTML5. Because of this, GameMaker is also compatible with them, which means that you can create a console experience for all sorts of games. Let's look at how GameMaker handles:

- ▶ Setting up a controller
- ▶ Utilizing analogue joystick acceleration

Touch controls

Touchscreens have been commercially available since 1983. Since then, the technology has come a long way and mobile devices, such as smartphones and tablets, have made touchscreens their primary mode of interaction. If you hope to get on the hundreds of games that are released for these platforms daily, you'll need to know a thing or two about touch controls. We'll learn about touch controls by:

- ▶ Adding tap control
- ▶ Using swipes

Tilt controls

Tilt controls are not always the best means of moving a character or object in a game but, used correctly and sparingly, can add much needed fun and excitement. This example will give you a good idea of how to create tilt controls for your game, but it's up to you to decide how (or if) you'll implement them. This includes the following:

- ▶ Moving characters or objects by tilting a device

Creating 2D movement

In *Chapter 1, Game Plan – Creating Basic Gameplay*, we demonstrated the basic character movement using GameMaker's drag and drop interface. It involved *a lot* of blocks. Next, we will create more sophisticated movement code in only a handful of code blocks.

Getting ready

You'll need a character object (`obj_player`) and a room where you can place it. We won't be discussing the object's sprite or animation here; this is purely about moving your character in two dimensions on the screen. For this reason, we're using a simple block to represent our player character.

How to do it...

1. In `obj_player`, add a **Create** event.

2. Drag and drop an **Execute Code** block (under the **Control** tab) into the Actions box.

3. Open it and enter the following code:

```
///set variables
max_spd = 12;
accel_spd = 1;
decel_spd = 2;
```

4. Close this code block and add a **Step** event.

5. Drag a code block to the **Actions** box and enter the following code:

```
///control movement
if (keyboard_check(vk_right)) and not (keyboard_check(vk_left))
{
hspeed += accel_spd;
hspeed = min(hspeed, max_spd);
}
if hspeed>0 and not (keyboard_check(vk_right))
{
hspeed -= decel_spd;
}
if (keyboard_check(vk_left)) and not (keyboard_check(vk_right))
{
hspeed -= accel_spd;
hspeed = max(hspeed, -max_spd);
}
if hspeed<0 and not (keyboard_check(vk_left))
{
hspeed += decel_spd;
}
if (keyboard_check(vk_left)) and (keyboard_check(vk_right)) or not
(keyboard_check(vk_left)) and not (keyboard_check(vk_right))
{
hspeed = 0;
}
```

6. Close this code block and you're done.

Placing / / / in front of the first line of code in a code block not only works like a comment (the compiler ignores it), it becomes the title of the code block and even appears in the **Actions** box. This is a great way to keep track of what each code block does.

How it works...

In the **Create** event, you need to set up a few variables that will be used only by your player character. These variables are then used in the `control movement` code block. This code tells GameMaker to check (every step) which keys are being pressed. If the right arrow key is being pressed but the left arrow key is not, the horizontal speed becomes equivalent to itself *plus* the value of acceleration (`accel_spd`) until the maximum speed (`max_spd`) is reached. Once the maximum speed is reached, if the player continues to hold the right arrow key, the character will continue to move at this speed. If the right arrow key is released, as long as the horizontal speed is greater than 0, the value of deceleration (`decel_spd`) is subtracted. This allows the character's acceleration and deceleration when moving, which is more realistic than jumping from 0 to top speed in an instant and vice versa. The last bit of code is simply used to make sure that if both left and right arrow keys are pressed simultaneously, the character will not move at all.

There's more...

The values used for each variable in this recipe are arbitrary, and you can choose your own values for each. If you're calculating a movement like this, I recommend that you play around with these values and playtest the results in order to make the character move in the way you want it to move.

See also

A basic character movement using GameMaker's drag and drop interface is discussed in *Chapter 1, Game Plan – Creating Basic Gameplay*.

Adding a Run button

One of my first "Aha!" moments in gaming as a kid was finding out that in *Super Mario Bros*, you could hold down the *B* button to make Mario run, allowing you to jump farther than a normal jump. Regardless of how you remember it, there was something exciting about moving that quickly, as though you were flying through this world by the seat of your pants. One false move and you were done for! Why not recreate that excitement by adding a *run* button of your own?

Getting ready

You'll need a character (`obj_player`) who has movement controls, at least horizontally. Refer to the code in the previous section if you need it.

How to do it...

1. Open `obj_player`.

2. Click on the **Step** event and open the `control movement` code block.

3. Below the movement code, add the following code:

```
//make the character run
if keyboard_check(vk_shift)
{
    hspeed = (hspeed*2);
}
```

That's it!

How it works...

This piece of code is simple as it is short. All it tells GameMaker to do is to check whether the player is holding the *Shift* key (it doesn't matter which one) and to double the horizontal speed as long as he or she is. This works in both directions without having to duplicate the code.

Making your character jump

Imagine that you grew up playing games, such as *Pitfall*, *Super Mario Bros*, or *Metroid* (it's likely the case for many of you). Now imagine playing these games without a jump button. You couldn't, could you? Of course not; these games feature jumping over obstacles and between platforms as a major gameplay element. Now, imagine you want to make your own platforming game. How would you make your character jump? Let's find out!

Getting ready

You'll need a character with movement controls, not unlike the ones you may have by following the preceding recipes. A jump animation is a good thing to have as well. It's not absolutely necessary, but I wrote the following code to incorporate one. You'll also need ground objects and any platforms you wish to have. You need to create one object with no sprite and call it `obj_ground_parent`. From there, you can create your platforms and ground objects with appropriate sprites, but make sure they all have `obj_ground_parent` listed as the parent. This way, when you program a collision for one, it associates with all of them.

How to do it...

1. In the **Create** event of `obj_player`, add the following variables:

    ```
    jump_spd = 15;
    grav = 1;
    grav_max = 10;
    ```

2. In the **Step** event, enter the following code above your movement code:

    ```
    if (!place_meeting(x, y+(vspeed/2), obj_ground_parent))
    {
        if vspeed < grav_max
        {
            vspeed+=grav;
        }
    }
    else
    {
        vspeed = 0;
    }
    ```

3. Enter this code *below* the existing movement code:

    ```
    //make the character jump
    if keyboard_check_pressed(vk_space) and (place_meeting(x,
    y+vspeed, obj_ground_parent))
    {
        vspeed = -jump_spd;
    }
    ```

4. Close the code block windows and you're done.

How it works...

With this code, you are essentially creating very basic gravity and then defying this gravity. The variables set in the **Create** event control your jump speed and gravity and the **Step** event code puts them to use.

The first line of code tells GameMaker that if your character is not currently in contact with the ground (or a platform), then its vertical speed will increase by the value of the gravity at every step, as long as the speed does not exceed the maximum value. This essentially creates a very basic form of velocity. If, however, your character is in contact with a platform or ground, the vertical speed is set to 0.

The next set of code is all you need for basic jump controls. You might notice that we're not checking whether the Spacebar key is being pressed, we're checking whether it was pressed. This is to prevent continuous jumping if the button is held down. If the player wants to jump again, he or she must press the button a second time. This will only work if the character is standing on the ground or platform, preventing the player from double jumping and beyond. You may also notice that the code used to actually make the player jump is the *negative* value of `jump_spd`. Simply put, this is because 0 on the *y* axis is at the *top* of the screen, as opposed to the bottom.

There's more...

By adding another variable (say, `djump`), you can allow your character to double jump:

1. Set the `djump` variable to a value of 1 in the **Create** event.

2. Replace your jump code with this code:

```
if keyboard_check_pressed(vk_space) and (place_meeting(x,
y+vspeed, obj_ground_parent))
{
    vspeed = -jump_spd;
    djump = 0;
}
else
{
    if keyboard_check_pressed(vk_space) and (djump < 1)
    {
        vspeed = -jump_spd;
        djump = 1;
    }
}
```

This code changes the value of `djump` to 0 when the player jumps while on the ground. So as long as the value of `djump` is less than 1, the player can jump again, but the code then changes `djump` back to 1, thereby disallowing a third jump.

See also

Physics will be discussed much more in depth in *Chapter 4, Let's Get Physical – Using GameMaker's Physics System*.

Using a point-and-click interface

If you've ever played a computer game, chances are you've done so using a mouse or similar device at one point or another. So many game genres utilize such a peripheral but few have made as big an impact as Diablo, which was released in 1996. Diablo was not the first action-RPG to use a mouse-based movement, but it was among the first to use 8 direction movement and certainly revitalized a game genre in decline. Even with the release of Diablo 3 in 2012, the biggest change is the 360-degree movement in place of the 8 direction movement based on a grid. Given the continued popularity of this genre, you may be inclined to recreate it in a game of your own, so let's do that now.

Getting ready

To start with, you'll need a room and an animated character set for either a top-down or 3/4 isometric view with separate sprites for each direction. This is easily achieved if you create a 3D model for your character and simply render out the various poses and animation frames, but this depends entirely on the visual style you choose for your game. Make sure to give each sprite a descriptive name such as `spr_player_walk_east`, `spr_player_walk_northeast`, and so on. Create one for each of the 8 directions. You'll also need two objects: one called `obj_player` using either one of the player walk sprites or a player idle sprite and one called `obj_waypoint` using a colored square sprite. `Obj_waypoint` should be invisible, though you can make it visible for testing purposes.

How to do it...

1. In `obj_player`, add a **Create** event.

2. Add a block of code containing the following code:

```
///set variables
speed = 0;
image_speed = 0;
waypoint = 0;
```

3. Add a **Step** event, where you'll drag two code blocks to the **Actions** box. The first block should contain this code:

```
///create waypoint
if mouse_check_button_pressed(mb_left) and waypoint = 0
{
    instance_create(mouse_x,mouse_y,obj_waypoint);
    waypoint = 1;
}
```

4. The second block will contain considerably more code than the first:

```
///player movement
if waypoint = 1
{
    move_towards_point(obj_waypoint.x, obj_waypoint.y, 5);
    image_speed = 1;
}
else
{
    speed=0;
}
if (direction >= 337.5 or direction < 22.5)
{
    sprite_index = spr_player_walk_east;
}
if (direction >= 22.5 and direction < 67.5)
{
    sprite_index = spr_player_walk_northeast;
}
...
```

There is much more to the code than I've added here, where you will see the ellipsis at the end. You should continue with the code for each of the 8 directions. Each direction should comprise 45 degrees without overlapping on adjacent directions.

5. Next, add a **Collision** event to `obj_waypoint` as the target.

6. Drag a code block to the **Actions** box and add the following code:

```
///stop player, remove waypoint
speed = 0;
waypoint = 0;
image_speed = 0;
    with obj_waypoint
{
    instance_destroy();
}
```

You can now test this (very basic) point-and-click movement, which is perfect for dungeon crawlers and action RPGs. If you make the waypoint visible, you can see when it is placed and removed, which will help you fine-tune the values to your liking.

How it works...

This code asks GameMaker to check various things at every step of the game. First, GameMaker checks whether `obj_waypoint` exists. If it does not exist, the player character does nothing; it stays right where it is. If you click anywhere in the room, however, this creates an instance of `obj_waypoint` and, since it now *does* exist, the character will walk toward it at a specified speed. GameMaker then checks which direction it's travelling in order to change the sprite to match that direction. Once it arrives at the *x* and *y* coordinates of `obj_waypoint`, GameMaker then removes the instance, causing the player character to stop in its tracks.

There's more...

Using this code as is will completely ignore all objects that *are not* `obj_waypoint`, so unless your character is a ghost that can walk through *anything*, you'll need to make sure it avoids solid objects. This can be done using GameMaker's drag and drop interface, specifically **Step Avoiding**, but you can fine-tune it to your liking by coding it yourself.

See also

Advanced movement and paths will be discussed further in *Chapter 3, Let's Move It – Advanced Movement and Layout*.

Following the cursor

As long as we're using the mouse, we may as well look into further uses for our favorite peripheral. Some games, like the brick breaker subgenre, may use the mouse without relying on the mouse buttons. As you move your mouse left and right, your paddle moves correspondently onscreen, allowing you to bounce a ball upwards toward bricks. You know... the ones you want to break. Tennis-style games like *Pong* work on the same basic principle, only on a different axis. If you've ever wanted to revisit this classic control scheme, now is as good a time as any.

Getting ready

We won't get into creating a full *Pong* or brick breaker style game at this point; we only want to learn how the paddle moves. In this case, we'll make a paddle that moves along the *x* axis. That said, all you need is a sprite and object named in the vein of `_paddle` and you're set.

How to do it...

Get ready for this one, it may take a while.

1. In `obj_paddle` add a **Step** event.

2. Place a code block in the **Actions** box and enter the following code:

```
///paddle movement
x = mouse_x;
```

Okay, you're finally done. Go grab some water and pat yourself on the back. You did it!

How it works...

With that one line of code (and one descriptive comment just in case you forget what it does) you've told GameMaker that you want the x coordinate for `obj_paddle` to be exactly that of your mouse cursor. That's all you need. It's not even necessary to code where the paddle should stop because GameMaker knows the size of the room; once the cursor leaves the confines of the room, it no longer exists. This type of control is great for brick breakers, *Pong* clones, or even balancing games, so use it at your own discretion.

There's more...

Okay, so you want to expand on this idea? How about something that follows the cursor at a slower pace? In the **Step** event, replace the code with this:

```
move_towards_point (mouse_x, mouse_y, 5);
```

This code will cause the object to constantly move toward the cursor's position. If you completed the previous recipe, you'd have used this code to make your player character move toward a mouse click. The difference here is that the x and y coordinates are dynamic, moving as the mouse moves without waiting for a click.

See also

We'll be looking into further uses for that mouse of yours in *Chapter 3, Let's Move It – Advanced Movement and Layout*.

Setting up a controller

Have you ever asked a gamer about his or her favorite gaming setup? Everyone has their preferences, but most gamers are very particular about how they control a game. Some gamers prefer a keyboard and mouse but other gamers, including myself, are quite fond of gamepads. If you check the history of game controllers, you might be surprised to find many variations. You may also be surprised to find how vehemently some gamers will defend their choice of input device, though many will tell you that it all comes down to what's comfortable. Personally, I prefer Xbox 360 and Xbox One controllers. Luckily, these are both compatible with the PC, so we will facilitate the use of one (and other compatible gamepads) in the next recipe.

Getting ready

You'll need at least one controller that can connect to your PC. Big surprise. I will use a wireless Xbox 360 controller that connects to my PC via a dedicated wireless dongle (I love this word; it's just fun to say). Your PC and GameMaker will do a lot of the work for you; we're just going to make coding for a gamepad a little easier.

How to do it...

Once you have your gamepad connected, it essentially works right away. I like to map the face buttons using a controller object that can be found in every room in the game.

1. Create an object with no sprite and call it `obj_control`.

2. Add a **Create** event and drag a code block to the **Actions** box.

3. Enter the following code in the code block:

```
///assign names to face buttons
gpad_A = gp_face1;
gpad_B = gp_face2;
gpad_X = gp_face3;
gpad_Y = gp_face4;
```

Close the code block and you're done.

How it works...

You may be wondering why I only chose to assign new variables to the four face buttons. The reason is that these are the only buttons for which GameMaker uses a nondescript name; all the other controls on the gamepad are named for what they are. For example, right on the D-pad becomes `gp_dpadr` and the **Select** button becomes `gp_select`. Buttons and controls such as these are universal across most, if not all, gamepads, whereas the face buttons have different designations based on the gamepad's manufacturer. For example, the **X** button on an Xbox controller would be the **Square** button on a PlayStation controller. You can rename any and all gamepad buttons in GameMaker but I find this to be quite unnecessary.

Once you have the buttons mapped to your liking, you can test them by putting the code in a **Step** event:

```
if gamepad_button_check_pressed(0, gpad_A)
{
  //your code here
}
```

This code will simply check whether the **A** button on the gamepad that is in the first controller slot has been pressed and released, and, if it has been pressed and released, it executes the commands.

Note that it is a best practice to verify that a gamepad is connected prior to using gamepad functions.

In the preceding case, you can nest the `if` statement in another `if` statement, as follows:

```
if gamepad_is_connected(0)
{
  global.gpad = true;
}
else
{
  global.gpad = false;
}
```

You can find more information at `http://docs.yoyogames.com/`.

Utilizing analogue joystick acceleration

Anyone who's used a modern gamepad controller knows that most games incorporate the joysticks for camera control and player movement, the latter being more common. Given this fact, it would be helpful to know how this works with GameMaker. Now, this can be handled by allowing GameMaker to check, in absolutes, whether one of the sticks is moving in a specific direction. This is fine for menus and the like, but what if you want to handle acceleration? Let's take a look at this.

Getting ready

Of course, you'll need to have at least one gamepad connected to your PC. It's not necessary to have the face buttons mapped, as seen in the previous recipe. You'll also need an object with a sprite to move with the gamepad, but this can simply be a box or any other sprite you have.

How to do it...

1. In your object, add a **Create** event to a code block.

2. In the code block, add the following code:

```
///set variables
max_spd = 12;
```

3. Now, add a **Step** event and drag a code block to the **Actions** box. The code block should contain the following code:

```
///analogue movement
if (gamepad_axis_value(0, gp_axislh) > 0.2) or (gamepad_axis_
value(0, gp_axislh) < (-0.2))
{
    hspeed = gamepad_axis_value(0, gp_axislh)*max_spd;
}
else
{
    hspeed = 0;
}
if (gamepad_axis_value(0, gp_axislv) > 0.2) or (gamepad_axis_
value(0, gp_axislv) < (-0.2))
{
    vspeed = gamepad_axis_value(0, gp_axislv)*max_spd;
}
```

```
    else
    {
        vspeed = 0;
    }
```

Here, you have a analogue movement with acceleration in all directions.

How it works...

This code may seem complicated, but it is really quite simple; the object's vertical and horizontal speeds are directly proportionate to the position of the left thumbstick. When a gamepad's thumbstick is used, GameMaker reads its position as a value between 1 and -1. Pushed all the way to the right, this value becomes one, but halfway to the right, this value becomes 0.5. As you can guess, the same value reads as -1 when pushed to the extreme left and 0 when at rest. Now, because GameMaker constantly checks the axis value and because thumbsticks can register every minute movement even when at rest, we created a "dead zone" that tells GameMaker to only increase the object's vertical or horizontal speed when the axis value reads within a specified range (which would require the player's physical input). This way, the object doesn't move around simply because you tilted your gamepad and gravity took over. Once the thumbstick is moved beyond this dead zone in any direction, the generated value is then multiplied by the maximum speed, which means that the object's speed is regulated by how far the thumbstick is pushed in that direction. See, its easy.

There's more...

You don't necessarily need to allow movement in all directions. If you ask GameMaker to check only for vertical or horizontal, it will only return the requested value, not both.

See also

Joystick movement will be discussed in *Chapter 3, Let's Move It – Advanced Movement and Layout*.

Adding tap control

If there's one thing mobile games and apps tell you to do, it's to tap something. Tap to start. Tap to continue. Tap to win! Okay, this one may be less common, but the point remains the same. Tap controls are the most common control styles in mobile games and the best part is they're not hard to code. Let's take a look at an example right now.

Getting ready

For this recipe, you'll need two objects. Give one object a simple sprite (such as a blue circle) and name it `obj_balloon` and name the other `obj_control` but don't assign a sprite to it. Make sure `obj_control` is placed inside the room you're using for this recipe.

How to do it...

1. In the control object, add a **Create** event to a code block that sets the following alarm:

    ```
    alarm[0] = 60;
    ```

2. Next, add an event to **Alarm0** using the following code:

    ```
    instance_create((random_range(0,room_width)),(random_range(0,room_
    height)),obj_balloon);
    ```

3. In `obj_balloon`, simply add a mouse left pressed event and enter this code into a code block:

    ```
    instance_destroy();
    obj_control.alarm[0] = 60;
    ```

That's it! Try running this on your mobile device or even on your computer, using the mouse to control.

How it works...

This recipe couldn't have been simpler, but it demonstrates an important point about how GameMaker utilizes touch controls. Here, your finger on the screen acts as the click of a mouse on your computer. Due to this correlation, the point-and-click interface, as seen previously, can be ported to a touchscreen device with few changes.

There's more...

The difference between a touchscreen and your computer is that most touchscreens can handle multi-touch, that is, multiple input points at the same time. Your computer isn't going to have multiple mice working simultaneously, so the standard functions don't work for multiple inputs. Instead of using the standard functions, you can use specific functions, such as `if device_mouse_check_button_pressed(0, mb_left) press=true;` where 0 represents the device being checked. Multi-touch can handle up to five inputs at one time, which are numbered 0-4. Keep this in mind if you're looking to use gestures for specific controls.

Using swipes

If you use a mobile device, such as a phone or tablet, it's a safe bet to use swipe controls in a game or an app; popular games such as *Fruit Ninja* have been designed entirely around this type of a touchscreen input. Swipe controls are intuitive for certain onscreen actions (such as slicing a fruit), so the game just *feels* right; it's *satisfying*. Let's take a moment to cook up some satisfying controls.

Getting ready

We'll create a simple demo to showcase the swipe movement. To do this, you'll need a simple room and two objects. The first object should be called `obj_target` and requires a sprite; I chose a simple green box. The second should be called `obj_control_swipe` and requires no sprite. Based on the name, I'm sure you can guess what this second object does.

How to do it...

1. In `obj_target`, add a **Create** event to a code block containing the following code:

```
x = room_width/2;
y = room_height/2;
```

2. Add a **Step** event to the code block where you'll enter this code:

```
if (x < 0) or (x > room_width) or (y < 0) or (y > room_height)
{
    instance_destroy();
    instance_create(room_width/2,room_height/2-50,obj_target);
}
```

3. This is all you'll need to do to the target, but make sure to add it to the room.

4. Next, open `obj_control_swipe` and add a **Create** event.

5. Drag a code block to the **Actions** tab and enter the following code:

```
mx_start = 0;
my_start = 0;
mx_end = 0;
my_end = 0;
swipe_time = 0;
swipe_speed = 0;
swipe = false;
```

6. When this is done, add a **Step** event to a code block containing the following code:

```
if mouse_check_button_pressed(mb_left)
{
    mx_start = mouse_x;
    my_start = mouse_y;
    swipe = true;
}
if swipe = true
{
    mx_end = mouse_x;
    my_end = mouse_y;
    swipe_time +=0.5;
    if mouse_check_button_released(mb_left)
    {
        swipe = false;
        swipe_speed = point_distance(mx_start,my_start,mx_end,my_
end)/swipe_time;
        swipe_time = 0;
        if collision_line(mx_start,my_start,mx_end,my_end,obj_
target,false,false)
        {
            with(obj_target)
            {
                direction = point_direction(other.mx_start, other.
my_start, other.mx_end, other.my_end);
                speed = other.swipe_speed;
            }
        }
    }
}
```

7. Close the control object and make sure you add it to your room. Though it is invisible, nothing will happen here without it. Once this is done, you're all set to test it.

How it works...

This recipe involves several conditional checks and `if` statements. As with any code, the reason is that we don't want certain things to happen unless certain prerequisites have been met. It first checks whether the left mouse button has been pressed, and if it has been pressed, it continues and sets the start coordinates of the mouse and the `swipe` variable to `true`. While `swipe` is true, GameMaker will track the mouse's coordinates and increase the value of `swipe_time` at every step. Once the left mouse button is released, `swipe` becomes `false` and the speed of the swipe is calculated. This is done by calculating the distance between the mouse button press and release, and dividing it by the current value of `swipe_time`, which is then set back to `0`.

Now, we don't want to move the target by swiping just anywhere, so we need GameMaker to check whether the target itself was swiped. This is done using `collision_line`, which takes the given start and end coordinates and checks whether the selected object collides with that line at any point. You must decide whether you want GameMaker to check the collision precisely, which is slower to compute (by entering `true`), or you can simply use the sprites collision mask, which is faster (by entering `false`). Here, we used the latter. You must check whether the calling instance (the object from which the code is read) should be excluded from the collision check or not by entering "true" to exclude it or "false" to include it. In this case, it was irrelevant.

Once all of these checks have been completed, if they all return *true*, GameMaker takes the speed (calculated previously) and the direction (set by checking the start and end coordinates of the swipe) and applies them to our target. So, based on how quickly you swipe and in which direction, as long as you connect to the target, it will move accordingly.

There's more...

As you may have guessed, moving the target isn't the most important part of this code; it's simply the outcome. You can use swipe gestures to do anything from the menu navigation to destroying enemies. Once the requirements to register a swipe have been completed, what that action does is completely up to you.

Moving characters or objects by tilting a device

Another widely used feature in smartphones and tablets is the built-in gyroscope. This component allows basic motion controls that are read by their movement. The most common use of device tilt is to control the screen's visual orientation, but it can also be used for games. We're going to take a look at how to use tilt controls to move an object around.

Getting ready

Before we begin, you'll need to set up your room for a mobile device. As we'll test tilt functions that utilize an accelerometer, this recipe can only be tested on a mobile device, such as a smartphone or tablet. With the purchase of a **GameMaker Professional license**, you can test them on Android devices without purchasing the exporter. If you wish to test on iOS or Windows mobile devices, you'll need to purchase their respective **export licenses**. For this recipe, I used the Android target in **portrait mode** for testing purposes. I set the room to 768 px wide by 1280 px high and locked the screen to portrait under **Global Game Settings**. You'll also need to create two objects: `obj_ball` and `obj_wall`. Give `obj_ball` a yellow circle as the sprite and make `obj_wall` a black square. Under **Object Properties** of `obj_wall`, make sure **Visible** is *not* checked.

In your room, place the ball anywhere within and surround the outer edge of the room with your wall object. For this purpose, you can either line the edges with individual instances of `obj_wall`, or simply use four of them that have been stretched to complete the perimeter.

How to do it...

1. Open `obj_ball` and add a **Step** event.

2. Drag a code block to the **Actions** box and add the following code:

```
if device_get_tilt_x() < -0.1 or device_get_tilt_x() > 0.1
{
        x -= (device_get_tilt_x()*20);
}
if device_get_tilt_y() < -0.1 or device_get_tilt_y() > 0.1
{
        y += (device_get_tilt_y()*20);
}
```

3. Now, add a **Collision** event to `obj_wall` as the target.

4. From the **Move** tab, drag the **Bounce** block to the **Actions** box and use the following settings:

```
Applies to: Self
Precise: Not precisely
Against: All objects
```

Once this is done, you can close all the boxes and test on your Android device by tilting it back and forth.

How it works...

For most devices, a tilt is registered by GameMaker using the device's accelerometer in the same way as it uses a gamepad's analogue joysticks. A value between 1 and -1 is populated based on how far the device is tilted in one direction. In some devices, a 90 degree tilt to the right produces a value of 1, whereas a 90 degree tilt to the left produces a value of -1. In other devices, this is reversed and the same goes for tilting up and down. If you test on your device and find that a tilt to the right sends the ball to the left, you can simply change `x -=...` to `x +=....`

The wall objects you placed in the room were simply used for testing purposes. Without them, your ball object can move outside the play area.

There's more...

This recipe calls for locking the device's screen orientation to Portrait mode. If you plan to make a game that has different control options depending on the device orientation, you can use the `display_get_orientation()` function. This function checks whether the device is in landscape or portrait mode or not and deploys your code accordingly. Refer to `http://docs.yoyogames.com/` for more information.

3
Let's Move It – Advanced Movement and Layout

In this recipe, we'll cover the following topics:

- Dragging onscreen objects
- Dragging objects on a grid
- Moving a character on a grid
- Setting a path
- Creating enemy pathfinding
- Controlling a character with a mouse and keyboard

Introduction

Ask any gamer what his/her favorite game is and you'll likely get an immediate response. Now ask the same gamer whether he/she would be willing to play only that game, and no other, forever. You probably won't get the same enthusiasm in the response and for good reason. I don't know about you, but I can't imagine playing just one game the rest of my life. Luckily, we have a lot of choice when it comes to what we play. With so many genres and subgenres out there, we end up with a limitless variety when it comes to games. Now, some developers create many games in the same genre; they've found a niche to fill and they're happy to do so. Others prefer to experiment with various genres, sometimes even combining aspects of multiple genres for a different experience.

If we didn't have games offering so many different experiences, we would get bored with games very quickly. It's up to developers to keep gaming fresh with new controls and gameplay styles, so we're going to take a look at how to recreate a few of these styles in GameMaker.

Drag and drop items/characters

Drag and drop controls work great in many situations, such as point-and-click adventures, strategy games, and even inventory systems. Let's make them happen in GameMaker.

- ▶ Dragging onscreen objects

Grid-based movements

Grids can be implemented in several different game styles, even when you might not be aware of them. Strategy games, puzzles, and RPGs can utilize grids to move characters and items around.

- ▶ Dragging objects on a grid
- ▶ Moving a character on a grid

Paths

GameMaker uses **paths** to allow several different gameplay elements. You can set enemies on a specific path to patrol a given area, you can create moving platforms and background elements, and you can even use them to move your players. Let's create some paths to see them in action:

- ▶ Setting a path
- ▶ Creating enemy pathfinding

Multiple inputs

Many mobile games utilize one-touch controls but how often do you see the same from PC and console games? With all of these buttons, there has to be *something* they can be used for right?

- ▶ Controlling a character with a mouse and keyboard

Dragging onscreen objects

Using your mouse to drag items onscreen is a common practice in many computer applications, and even predates the release of Windows 3.1, which brought the visual interface into the mainstream. If you use a computer for work or play, you certainly drag icons, text, and so on on a daily basis; you even do it when creating with GameMaker. Dragging items has many applications in games, but in order to implement it, we first need to know how it works.

Getting ready

You'll need a room and an object called `obj_block` to place in it. The sprite can be anything here, so I've simply made a blue square. Place the object anywhere in the room and you're ready to go.

How to do it

1. In `obj_block`, add a **Create** event.

2. Drag and drop a code block using the following code:

```
///Set variables
dragged = false;
global.canDrag = true;
```

3. Add a **Left Button** event.

4. Drag a code block to the **Actions** box and enter the following code:

```
///Pick up object
if global.canDrag = true
{
    global.canDrag = false;
    dragged = true;
}
```

5. Add a **Step** event.

6. In this event, place a code block using the following code:

```
///Drag object
if dragged = true
{
    x = mouse_x;
    y = mouse_y;
}
```

7. Add a **Global Left Released** event (under **Mouse | Global Mouse**).

8. Drop a code block in the **Actions** box using this code:

```
///Drop object
dragged = false;
global.canDrag = true;
```

Once this is done, you can test your code. Try it with multiple instances of `obj_block` in the same room.

How it works

As you can see, the **Create** event sets the two variables that will be used to tell GameMaker whether an object can be picked up and dragged around with the mouse or not. The variable dragged checks whether the left mouse button is being pressed. We tell GameMaker to set the *x* and *y* coordinates of the object to be represented by the appropriate coordinates of the mouse, as long as dragged is `true`. Since the code for this is in a **Step** event, once the left mouse button is released and dragged becomes `false`, the object then ignores the mouse's *x* and *y* coordinates and stays put (unless told to do otherwise).

You may have also noticed that the `canDrag` variable is a global variable. This is used to prevent the mouse from picking up other objects if the player drags something on top of them. While the dragged variable pertains to the specific object being dragged, the `canDrag` global variable pertains to everything in the game. This way, as long as an object is being dragged around, no other object can be picked up. Now, you can obviously change this if you want a mouse drag to pick up multiple objects, but keep in mind that this code will stack objects in *exactly* the same place. This means that multiple instances of the same object will appear to become one.

Dragging objects on a grid

Often, games require objects to be in specific locations in order to be used, such as buildings in a real-time strategy game. When placing your building, you'll need to drop it on a specific grid. There are different ways to demonstrate this, but the most common way is simply to lock the building to the said grid in order to keep it from being placed in an undesired location. If real life worked this way, then construction planning would be a breeze. Since real life does *not* work like this, let's at least make it happen in GameMaker so that we can enjoy some form of worry-free construction.

Getting ready

This recipe assumes the completion of the previous recipe, *Dragging onscreen objects*, so you'll need to get it done and open your GameMaker file. Go ahead and do it now, if you haven't; I'll wait. All set? Good. Now before you begin, there are certain things you need to check. Make sure the length and width of the room you're using is divisible by 32. If you wish to use a different value, this should be reflected in the given equation. I used 1024 x 768. For testing purposes, you may wish to create a simple grid background in order to see the snapping in action. Again, the grid needs to match the equation you use.

How to do it

1. Open the **Object Properties** of `obj_block`.
2. Under the **Step** event, open the code block labeled `Drag object`.
3. Replace the code for the *x* and *y* coordinates with the following code:

```
x=(mouse_x div 32)*32 +16;
y=(mouse_y div 32)*32 +16;
```

Once this is completed, you can test it by picking up a block and moving it around. Notice that it will not even appear between the grid points. This means that you can drop it anywhere and it will always be within the confines of the grid.

How it works

This code works just like the code in the previous section, but it restricts the object's movement in order to keep it within the confines of the grid. This way, the object will never be out of place. Essentially, you're telling GameMaker that when `obj_block` is picked up, it can only be moved along the grid by means of the equations used to establish its *x* and *y* coordinates. For *x*, we use the `div` function to take the numerical value of the mouse's position on the *x* axis, divide it by 32, and round it to the nearest whole integer. This new value is then multiplied by 32 to give the resemblance of an actual grid position, and 16 is added to the center of the object in a single box on the grid, 16 being half of 32.

Now, in this case, we haven't actually built a grid in the game. We're causing the object to move as though it is bound by a grid, but GameMaker does not keep track of what objects lie in each space; that's for another recipe.

Moving a character on a grid

As you may have guessed so far, a lot of games use grids for various purposes. We've seen moving objects around a grid with the mouse, but what you may not realize is that many games that use keys or a controller for movements also utilize grids. Classic role playing and action games, such as the original *Legend of Zelda* or *Pokemon*, keep the player on a grid in order to force players into specific positions or to facilitate the environment layout. Let's take a look at how to use a grid to move a player smoothly.

Getting ready

To begin, you'll need four sprites and an object called `obj_player`. Each sprite will represent a direction of travel: right, left, up, and down. If your character is symmetrical, you can simply flip one sprite horizontally. Make sure that you use a descriptive naming convention for your sprites; I chose `spr_player_move_right`, and so on. Assign one of these sprites to the object itself to begin with and you're ready to go.

How to do it

1. Open `obj_player` and add a **Create** event.

2. Drag a code block to the **Actions** box and enter the following code:

```
///set destination
image_speed = 0;
destination_x = x;
destination_y = y;
walking = false;
```

3. Add a **Step** event.

4. In a code block, enter the following code:

```
///walk or do not walk
if (destination_x == x and destination_y == y)
{
    walking = false;
    image_speed = 0;
}
```

5. Enter this code and complete it for the *x* and *y* axes:

```
///character direction and movement
if (destination_x > x)
{
    x +=2
```

```
}
if (destination_x < x)
{
    x -=2
}
...
```

6. In the same code block, enter this code and complete the movement in all directions:

```
if (keyboard_check(vk_right) and not walking)
{
    destination_x += 32;
    image_speed = 1;
    sprite_index = spr_player_move_right;
    walking = true;
}
if (keyboard_check(vk_left) and not walking)
{
    destination_x -= 32;
    image_speed = 1;
    sprite_index = spr_player_move_left;
    walking = true;
}
...
```

Now, you can place your player object in the room and test it. You can press any direction key and the player will move to the next available space along the grid. Hold down the key and the player will keep moving!

How it works

The previous recipe can potentially be executed in several ways. This way offers a smooth movement while sticking to a grid and can be adjusted for speed preferences. By setting the `destination_` variables, you're allowing the player to give GameMaker the coordinates of the next grid space to which he or she would like to move, assuming that the player is not already moving. The code then tells GameMaker that once this destination is set, you need to move the player object at a set speed in pixels per step. While this is going on, the `walking` variable tells GameMaker that the player is just walking. While the player is walking, GameMaker no longer sets the destination, but once the previously set destination is reached, walking once again becomes false and GameMaker can set a new destination, assuming that the player is still holding a direction key. The grid size and the speed at which the player object moves are arbitrary and will depend on your preferences. One thing to keep in mind, though, is that the grid size must be divisible by the speed, otherwise your player object will end up moving independent of the grid.

There's more...

You may have noticed that while the character is moving, we used the walking variable. This would imply that there is more than one mode of transportation (think of the bicycle in Pokemon). With the use of another variable and some more if statements, you can have variable speeds for your player's movement, which is similar to the **Run** button in *Chapter 1, Game Plan – Creating Basic Gameplay*.

Setting a path

In GameMaker, paths can be used for many things, some of which will be discussed in the following recipes. Before we get started with the recipes, it might be helpful to first learn how to create simple paths and move objects along them.

Getting ready

Before we make a path, let's take a quick look at the tool itself. To open the path editor, click on the icon at the top of the window that looks like a green arrow moving in a serpentine fashion.

This will open a window where you can plot the path, straight or curved, to be used in your game.

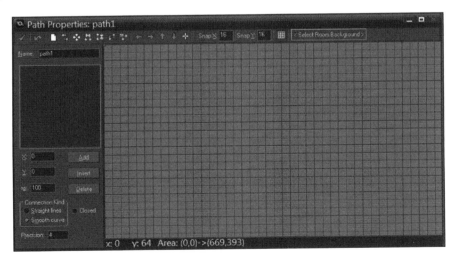

Name the path, `path_test`.

How to do it

1. With the path editor open, select **Smooth Curve**.

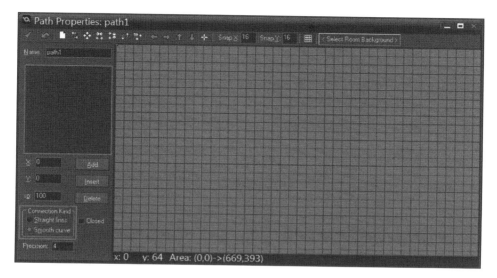

2. Uncheck the box marked **Closed**.

3. Click on the grid to place the first point of your path.

4. Place two more path points along the same x axis.

5. Now that the second point has turned blue, you can alter the curve of the path. Move this point up in order to create an upwards curve.

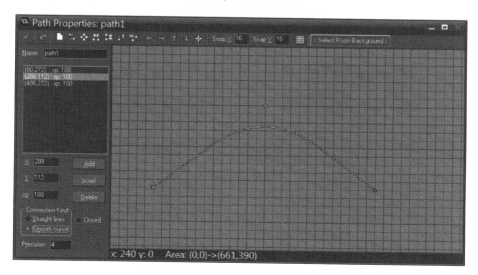

6. Continue with the path by adding more points and adjusting the curves of each section.

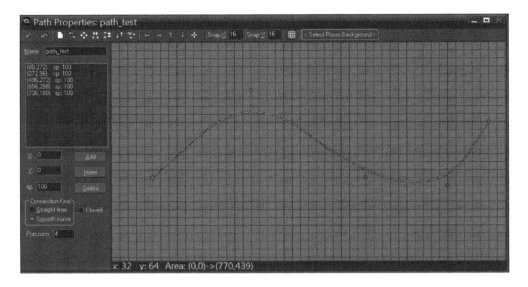

7. Save your path and create a new object called `obj_path_test`.

8. Give this new object a red square for the sprite and add a **Create** event.

9. Drag **Set Path** from the **Move** tab to the **Actions** box.

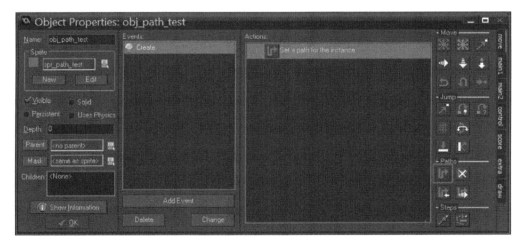

10. In **Set Path**, use the following settings:

    ```
    Applies to: Self
    Path: path_test
    Speed: 5
    At end: Reverse
    Relative: Relative
    ```

11. Place an instance of `obj_path_test` anywhere in the room.

When you test your game, `obj_path_test` will follow the path you created, though you won't be able to see the actual path. You can edit any path you create, allowing you to tweak it to your needs.

How it works

Paths are very simple to set up, but very versatile when applied to your game. By adding more points and adjusting the angle of each curve, you can move objects exactly how you want to move them and where you need them. Adjusting the numerical value of **Precision** will change according to how precisely the path follows the curve you created by adding or removing vertices along the line. You can alter this value on a scale of 1 to 8, 1 being straight lines and sharp angles, 8 being much softer curves.

On the left-hand side of the editor window, you will see each point on the path as well as its coordinates. You can use the buttons here to add a point to the line, insert a point before the selected point, or delete the selected point. You can also select each point after you've plotted it and alter its *x* and *y* coordinates as well as its relative speed at that point in the path (sp). Play around with the points and values here to see what kind of a path you can create.

There's more

Once you've created a path, you can use the **Path Editor** to alter the line, resize the path, mirror it, flip it, and rotate it, as well as shift its position. When you use the path with an object, I recommend that you test it with different settings in the **Set Path** options box. Changing the speed yields predictable results, but try the others. You can allow your object to reverse its path when it reaches the end, like we did here, but you can also allow it to stop, start over from the beginning of the path, or continue from the end. Changing the **Relative** setting from relative to absolute will cause GameMaker to ignore your placement of the object in the room and instead follow the coordinates of each point as they were in the editor (this can change the path's size as well as its location). Try them all out!

Creating enemy pathfinding

In games, there are several ways to move enemies around the playable area. In *Chapter 1, Game Plan – Creating Basic Gameplay*, we discussed a simple way of using the *x* and *y* coordinates. In the previous recipe, we discussed setting paths, which can also be used to shuttle enemies around the screen for your player to avoid or destroy. These are both good options, depending on what you want for your game, but what about enemies that can actually navigate a level, avoid obstacles, and pursue the player? Let's add some depth to a top-down game by creating a slightly more complex enemy AI.

Getting ready

First, you'll need a character object called obj_player that can move in four directions (with collision detection), and an enemy object called obj_enemy. Once again, I've animated the player character using the 3/4 top-down sprites from previous recipes. For the enemy sprite, though, let's take a red circle and add a line (the one with the arrow) to the right side of the image so that you can see which direction the enemy is facing.

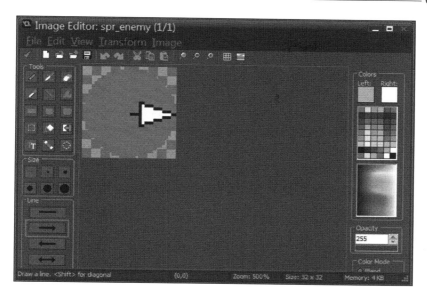

You'll also need an object called `obj_wall` for your enemy to navigate. Make the wall a 32 x 32 pixel block and set the origin to (0,0). Place it around the border of your room and use it to create a sort of labyrinth throughout. Before you do this, make sure that your room has dimensions that are divisible by 32.

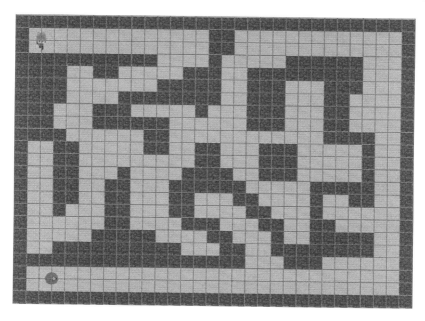

How to do it

1. In `obj_player`, add a **Create** event.

2. Place a code block in the **Actions** box and add the following:

    ```
    image_speed = 0;
    ```

3. Add a **Step** event with a code block.

4. Enter the following code:

    ```
    ///player movement and collision detection
    if (keyboard_check(vk_right)) and (!place_meeting((x + 8), y, obj_
    wall))
    {
        sprite_index = spr_player_move_right;
        image_speed = 1;
        x += 8;
    }
    else if (keyboard_check(vk_left)) and (!place_meeting((x - 8), y,
    obj_wall))
    {
        sprite_index = spr_player_move_left;
        image_speed = 1;
        x -= 8;
    }
    else if (keyboard_check(vk_up)) and (!place_meeting(x, (y - 8),
    obj_wall))
    {
        sprite_index = spr_player_move_up;
        image_speed = 1;
        y -= 8;
    }
    else if (keyboard_check(vk_down)) and (!place_meeting(x, (y + 8),
    obj_wall))
    {
        sprite_index = spr_player_move_down;
        image_speed = 1;
        y += 8;
    }
    else
    {
        image_speed = 0;
    }
    ```

5. Open `obj_enemy` and add a **Step** event.

6. Drag a code block to the **Actions** box and add the following:

```
///enemy pathfinding
image_angle = direction
room_grid = mp_grid_create(0,0,room_width/32,room_
height/32,32,32);
enemy_path = path_add();
mp_grid_add_instances(room_grid, obj_wall, 1);
mp_grid_path(room_grid, enemy_path, x, y, obj_player.x, obj_
player.y, 1)
path_start(enemy_path, 5, "", 1);
```

Your enemy object is now ready to track down your player object. The hunt is on!

How it works

The movement code in this recipe doubles as collision detection for the player object. Using `!place_meeting(x, y, object)` allows you to move the character *only* if an instance of `obj_wall` is not currently in the space to which you wish to move. This means that GameMaker will look at the coordinates you provide (current *x* coordinate and current *y* coordinate plus 8 pixels, for example) to see whether or not an instance of `obj_wall` is there. If the coast is clear, you are okay to move in that direction. If `obj_wall` is there, then GameMaker will not execute the movement code.

The pathfinding code works well to have one or many objects follow another without clipping through other objects but it assumes one thing: The enemy knows where the player is at all times. This isn't ideal for creating realistic enemy AI, but it does demonstrate the use of a **Motion Planning** grid, or `mp_grid`. Motion planning is a series of functions that allows GameMaker to plot a course for an object using various means. In this case, we used the more elaborate **Motion Planning** grid, which uses a grid that you plot in a given area to decide the best path for the object to reach its goal. We've used the entire room as a given space, created a 32 x 32 virtual grid, and instructed the enemy object to use this grid to plot 8-directional movement in order to find the player while avoiding the walls. Once the grid is set and the instructions are given, we've used `path_start` to begin the hunt. Notice the quotation marks? That space is reserved for the path's end action. By assigning a number from 0-3 you can tell the enemy, assuming it reaches its target, to either end the path, continue from the starting position, continue from its current position, or go backwards across the path. Here, because we want the enemy to continue hunting the player, we've given an empty string, meaning neither of those four actions apply. Be sure to play around with these options, as well as grid size and targets, until you find an AI that works for you.

There's more...

In order for this code to work smoothly, you'll need to make sure your player object is unable to clip through the wall objects. As mentioned previously, the movement code we used creates a very simple collision detection that prevents `obj_player` from moving through solid objects. Code like this is important because if your player is occupying the same space as an object the enemy is programmed to avoid, the enemy will deem that the player no longer exists. This can result in the enemy stopping its path, but can also cause errors or glitches, such as disappearing enemy objects.

See also

You can read more about **Motion Planning** at `http://docs.yoyogames.com/`.

Controlling a character with a mouse and keyboard

In the previous chapter, we looked at how to control your player character with a mouse, as well as a keyboard. I'm willing to bet you've played a game that required an input from both of these devices at the *same time*. You have, haven't you? I thought so. Let's take a look at a classic gameplay element that requires multiple inputs to shoot aliens.

Getting ready

We need a hero. Not an *actual* hero, mind you, but rather a player character who can run around onscreen and shoot things. For the purposes of this recipe, we'll use a static image of a guy with a gun, seen from the top. Let's turn it into a sprite called `spr_player` and use it to represent an object of the same name. You'll also need a sprite called `spr_alien`, which should be an image of an alien, also seen from above. Use this sprite to represent `obj_alien`. You'll need a controller object to spawn aliens, so we'll call it `obj_alien_controller`. To make this more of a game, let's create bullets so that our hero can take care of the alien horde and save the world. Create a small bullet sprite called `spr_bullet` and an object following the same name.

How to do it

1. Open `obj_player` and add a **Step** event.
2. Drag a code block to the **Actions** box and add the following code:

```
///keyboard movement
if keyboard_check(ord('W')) && (y>=32)
```

```
{
    y -= 5;
}
if keyboard_check(ord('S')) && (y<=(room_height-32))
{
    y += 5;
}
if keyboard_check(ord('A')) && (x>=32)
{
    x -= 5;
}
if keyboard_check(ord('D')) && (x<=(room_width-32))
{
    x += 5;
}
```

3. Drag a second code block to the **Actions** box and enter the following code:

```
///player rotation
direction = point_direction(x,y,mouse_x,mouse_y);
image_angle = direction;
if mouse_check_button_pressed(mb_left)
{
    instance_create(x, y, obj_bullet);
}
```

4. Close `obj_player` and open `obj_alien`.

5. Create a **Step** event and drag a code block to the **Actions** box.

6. Enter the following code:

```
///follow player
move_towards_point(obj_player.x, obj_player.y, 3);

image_angle = point_direction(x, y, obj_player.x, obj_player.y);
```

7. Create a **Collision** event using `obj_bullet`.

8. Drag a code block to the **Actions** box and add the following code:

```
///destroy alien and bullet
instance_destroy();
with(other)
{
  instance_destroy();
}
```

9. Close `obj_alien` and open `obj_bullet`.

10. Add a **Create** event and drag a code block to the **Actions** box.

11. Enter the following code before closing `obj_bullet`:

```
///bullet trajectory
direction = obj_player.direction;
speed = 10;
```

12. Create an object called `obj_alien_controller`. Do not give it a sprite.

13. In `obj_alien_controller`, add a **Create** event.

14. Drag a code block to the **Actions** box and add the following code:

```
///set alarm
spawn = 0;
alarm[0] = 180;
```

15. Add an event to `Alarm0`.

16. Drag a code block to the **Actions** box and add the following code:

```
///set spawn switch
spawn = 1;
spawn_point = choose(0,1,2,3);
alarm[0] = 120;
```

17. Create a **Step** event and drag a code block to the **Actions** box.

18. Add the following code:

```
///spawn aliens
if spawn = 1
{
spawn = 0;
if (spawn_point = 0)
{
    instance_create(-64,random(room_height), obj_alien);
}
if (spawn_point = 1)
{
    instance_create((room_width+64), random(room_height), obj_
alien);
}
if (spawn_point = 2)
{
```

```
        instance_create(random(room_width), -64, obj_alien);
    }
    if (spawn_point = 3)
    {
        instance_create(random(room_width), (room_height+64), obj_
    alien);
    }
}
```

Once these steps are completed, you can close the controller object and it is ready to go. Make sure that there is an instance each of `obj_alien_controller` and `obj_player` in the room and press play to test it.

How it works

This recipe essentially puts to use elements of previous recipes we've looked at. The movement code is not different from what we've used, though we've moved it to incorporate the WASD key formation. Using the `point_direction` function, we allow the player to constantly face your mouse's position, making aiming quick and easy. This control style is great for top-down shooters, sometimes called *bullet hell* games if they're really fast-paced and intense.

The aliens, as you may have guessed, are being spawned by the alien controller object. By asking it to choose from a list of four choices, we can have it spawn along any side of the room at a random place. Using the `move_towards_point` function in the alien's Step event, we can ensure that any alien that spawns is immediately set to run toward our player, even as he moves around the room. That is, until he shoots them, at least. You can also use *multiple* controller objects as spawn points if you'd like to avoid using random values. Simply, tell the controller to spawn at its location, place them wherever you want, and you're off.

With these elements put together, you more or less have yourself a game. You can add a score, crosshairs for your mouse, player health, and many more to make it look more like the games that we know, but here you have the basics. Let's see what you can do with it.

There's more

Now, if you prefer to use a gamepad, this same style could translate into a twin-stick shooter. Instead of having the player's movement and direction linked directly to key presses and the position of the mouse, you can assign them to the analogue sticks on a gamepad. We've looked at moving a player around with one stick, and rotating the player using a second is quite similar.

Since the analogue stick's output is read as values along the horizontal and vertical axis, we'll need to use them to tell GameMaker exactly where our player should be looking:

```
var h_val = gamepad_axis_value(pad_num, gp_axisrh);
var v_val = gamepad_axis_value(pad_num, gp_axisrv);
if ((h_val != 0) or (v_val != 0))
{
direction = point_direction(0, 0, h_val, v_val);
image_angle = direction;
}
```

Here, we tell GameMaker to read both the vertical and horizontal axis of the right analogue stick and check whether they are equal to 0 or not. Assuming that one or both values is not 0, GameMaker takes the values recorded and plugs them into the `point_direction` function, which is similar to using the mouse's x and y coordinates. From there, we simply need to equate the player's direction and image angle to the `point_direction` function and the player will follow the movement of the right analogue stick.

One important caveat to this is that without a proper "deadzone", you may see some movement errors. Analogue sticks can move about slightly without the user applying any pressure. For this, we can set parameters such that it does not act on the input below a certain level, as we did in a previous recipe. For this case, I would recommend that you set the deadzone using the following code:

```
gamepad_set_axis_deadzone(pad, 0.5);
```

See also

Spawn points and emitters will be discussed further in *Chapter 9, Particle Man, Particle Man – Adding Polish to Your Game with Visual Effects and Particles*.

4
Let's Get Physical – Using GameMaker's Physics System

In this chapter, we'll cover the following topics:

- ▸ Creating objects that use physics
- ▸ Alternating gravity
- ▸ Applying force via magnets
- ▸ Creating a moving platform
- ▸ Making a rope

Introduction

The majority of video games are ruled by physics in one way or another. 2D platformers require coded movement and jump physics. Shooters, both 2D and 3D, use ballistic calculators that vary in sophistication to calculate whether you shot that guy or missed him and he's still coming to get you. Even *Pong* used rudimentary physics to calculate the ball's trajectory after bouncing off of a paddle or wall. The next time you play a 3D shooter or action-adventure game, check whether or not you see the logo for Havok, a physics engine used in over 500 games since it was introduced in 2000. The point is that physics, however complex, is important in video games. GameMaker comes with its own engine that can be used to recreate physics-based sandbox games, such as *The Incredible Machine*, or even puzzle games, such as *Cut the Rope* or *Angry Birds*. Let's take a look at how elements of these games can be accomplished using GameMaker's built-in physics engine.

Physics engine 101

In order to use GameMaker's physics engine, we first need to set it up. Let's create and test some basic physics before moving on to something more complicated.

▸ Creating objects that use physics

Gravity and force

One of the things that we learned with regards to GameMaker physics was to create our own simplistic gravity. Now that we've set up gravity using the physics engine, let's see how we can bend it to our will.

▸ Alternating gravity

▸ Applying force via magnets

Physics in the environment

GameMaker's physics engine allows you to choose not only the objects that are affected by external forces but also allows you to see how they are affected. Let's take a look at how this can be applied to create environmental objects in your game.

▸ Creating moving platforms

Advanced physics-based objects

Many platforming games, going all the way back to *Pitfall!*, have used objects, such as a rope as a gameplay feature. *Pitfall!*, mind you, uses static rope objects to help the player avoid crocodiles, but many modern games use dynamic ropes and chains, among other things, to create a more immersive and challenging experience.

▸ Making a rope

Creating objects that use physics

There's a trend in video games where developers create products that are less games than play areas; worlds and simulators in which a player may or may not be given an objective and it wouldn't matter either way. These games can take on a life of their own; *Minecraft* is essentially a virtual game of building blocks and yet has become a genre of its own, literally making its creator, Markus Persson (also known as Notch), a billionaire in the process. While it is difficult to create, the fun in games such as *Minecraft* is designed by the player. If you give a player a set of tools or objects to play with, you may end up seeing an outcome you hadn't initially thought of and that's a good thing. The reason why I have mentioned all of this is to show you how it ties to GameMaker and what we can do with it. In a sense, GameMaker is a lot like *Minecraft*. It is a set of tools, such as the physics engine we're about to use, that the user can employ if he/she desires (within limits, of course), in order to create something funny or amazing or both.

What you do with these tools is up to you, but you have to start somewhere. Let's take a look at how to build a simple physics simulator.

Getting ready

The first thing you'll need is a room. Seems simple enough, right? Well, it is. One difference, however, is that you'll need to enable physics before we begin. With the room open, click on the **Physics** tab and make sure that the box marked **Room is Physics World** is checked.

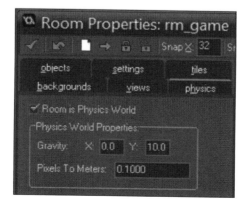

After this, we'll need some sprites and objects. For sprites, you'll need a circle, triangle, and two squares, each of a different color. The circle is for `obj_ball`. The triangle is for `obj_poly`. One of the squares is for `obj_box`, while the other is for `obj_ground`. You'll also need four objects without sprites: `obj_staticParent`, `obj_dynamicParent`, `obj_button`, and `obj_control`.

How to do it

1. Open `obj_staticParent` and add two collision events: one with itself and one with `obj_dynamicParent`.

2. In each of the collision events, drag and drop a comment from the **Control** tab to the **Actions** box.

3. In each comment, write `Collision`.

4. Close `obj_staticParent` and repeat steps 1-3 for `obj_dynamicParent`.

5. In `obj_dynamicParent`, click on **Add Event**, and then click on **Other** and select **Outside Room**.

6. From the **Main1** tab, drag and drop **Destroy Instance** in the **Actions** box. Select **Applies to Self**.

7. Open `obj_ground` and set the parent to `obj_staticParent`.

8. Add a **Create** event with a code block containing the following code:

```
var fixture = physics_fixture_create();
physics_fixture_set_box_shape(fixture, sprite_width / 2, sprite_height / 2);
physics_fixture_set_density(fixture, 0);
physics_fixture_set_restitution(fixture, 0.2);
physics_fixture_set_friction(fixture, 0.5);
physics_fixture_bind(fixture, id);
physics_fixture_delete(fixture);
```

9. Open the room that you created and start placing instances of `obj_ground` around it to create platforms, stairs, and so on. This is how mine looked like:

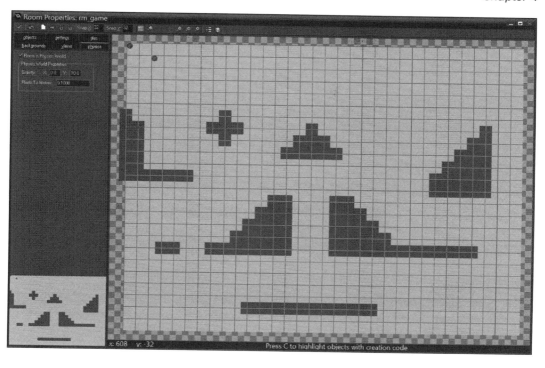

10. Open `obj_ball` and set the parent to `obj_dynamicParent`.

11. Add a **Create** event and enter the following code:

```
var fixture = physics_fixture_create();
physics_fixture_set_circle_shape(fixture, sprite_get_width(spr_
ball) / 2);
physics_fixture_set_density(fixture, 0.25);
physics_fixture_set_restitution(fixture, 1);
physics_fixture_set_friction(fixture, 0.5);
physics_fixture_bind(fixture, id);
physics_fixture_delete(fixture);
```

12. Repeat steps 10 and 11 for `obj_box`, but use this code:

```
var fixture = physics_fixture_create();
physics_fixture_set_box_shape(fixture, sprite_width / 2, sprite_
height / 2);
physics_fixture_set_density(fixture, 0.5);
physics_fixture_set_restitution(fixture, 0.2);
physics_fixture_set_friction(fixture, 0.01);
physics_fixture_bind(fixture, id);
physics_fixture_delete(fixture);
```

13. Repeat steps 10 and 11 for `obj_poly`, but use this code:

```
var fixture = physics_fixture_create();
physics_fixture_set_polygon_shape(fixture);
physics_fixture_add_point(fixture, 0, -(sprite_height / 2));
physics_fixture_add_point(fixture, sprite_width / 2, sprite_height
/ 2);
physics_fixture_add_point(fixture, -(sprite_width / 2), sprite_
height / 2);
physics_fixture_set_density(fixture, 0.01);
physics_fixture_set_restitution(fixture, 0.1);
physics_fixture_set_linear_damping(fixture, 0.5);
physics_fixture_set_angular_damping(fixture, 0.01);
physics_fixture_set_friction(fixture, 0.5);
physics_fixture_bind(fixture, id);
physics_fixture_delete(fixture);
```

14. Open `obj_control` and add a **Create** event using the following code:

```
globalvar shape_select;
globalvar shape_output;
shape_select = 0;
```

15. Add a **Step** and add the following code to a code block:

```
if mouse_check_button(mb_left) && alarm[0] < 0 && !place_
meeting(x, y, obj_button)
{
instance_create(mouse_x, mouse_y, shape_output);
alarm[0] = 5;
}
if mouse_check_button_pressed(mb_right)
{
    shape_select += 1;
}
```

16. Now, add an event to `alarm[0]` and give it a comment stating `Set Timer`.

17. Place an instance of `obj_control` in the room that you created, but make sure that it is placed in the coordinates (0, 0).

18. Open `obj_button` and add a **Step** event.

19. Drag a code block to the **Actions** tab and input the following code:

```
if shape_select > 2
{
    shape_select = 0;
}
if shape_select = 0
{
    sprite_index = spr_ball;
    shape_output = obj_ball;
}
if shape_select = 1
{
    sprite_index = spr_box;
    shape_output = obj_box;
}
if shape_select = 2
{
    sprite_index = spr_poly;
    shape_output = obj_poly;
}
```

Once these steps are completed, you can test your physics environment. Use the right mouse button to select the shape you would like to create, and use the left mouse button to create it. Have fun!

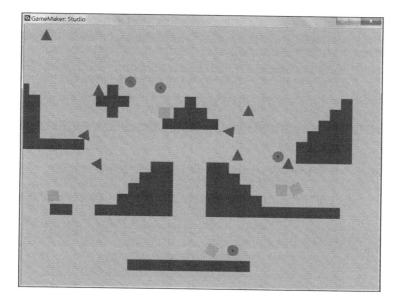

How it works

While not overly complicated, there is a fair amount of activity in this recipe. Let's take a quick look at the room itself. When you created this room, you checked the box for **Room is Physics World**. This does exactly what it says it does; it enables physics in the room. If you have any physics-enabled objects in a room that is not a physics world, errors will occur. In the same menu, you have gravity settings (which are vector-based) and pixels to meters, which sets the scale of objects in the room. This setting is important as it controls how each object is affected by the coded physics. YoYo Games based GameMaker's physics on the real world (as they should) and so GameMaker needs to know how many meters are represented by each pixel. The higher the number, the larger the world in the room. If you place an object in two different rooms with different pixel to meter settings, even though the objects have the same settings, GameMaker will apply physics to them differently because it views them as being of differing size and weight.

Let's take a look at the objects in this simulation. Firstly, you have two parent objects: one static and the other dynamic. The static object is the only parent to one object: `obj_ground`. The reason for this is that static objects are not affected by outside forces in a physics world, that is, the room you built. Because of this, the ground pieces are able to ignore gravity and forces applied by other objects that collide with them. Now, neither `obj_staticParent` nor `obj_dynamicParent` contain any physics code; we saved this for our other objects. We use our parent objects to govern our collision groups using two objects instead of coding collisions in each object. So, we use drag and drop collision blocks to ensure that any children can collide with instances of one another and with themselves. Why did you drag comment blocks into these collision events? We did this so that GameMaker doesn't ignore them; the contents of each comment block are irrelevant. Also, the dynamic parent has an event that destroys any instance of its children that end up outside the room. The reason for this is simply to save memory. Otherwise, each object, even those off-screen, would be accounted for in calculations at every step and this would slow everything down and eventually crash the program.

Now, as we're using physics-enabled objects, let's see how each one differs from the others. When working with the object editor, you may have noticed the checkbox labelled **Uses Physics**. This checkbox will automatically set up the basic physics code within the selected object, but only after assuming that you're using the drag and drop method of programming. If you click on it, you'll see a new menu with basic collision options as well as several values and associated options:

> ▶ **Density**: Density in GameMaker works exactly as it does in real life. An object with a high density will be much heavier and harder to move via force than a low-density object of the same size. Think of how far you can kick an empty cardboard box versus how far you can kick a cardboard box full of bricks, assuming that you don't break your foot.

- **Restitution**: Restitution essentially governs an object's bounciness. A higher restitution will cause an object to bounce like a rubber ball, whereas a lower restitution will cause an object to bounce like a box of bricks, as mentioned in the previous example.

- **Collision group**: Collision grouping tells GameMaker how certain objects react with one another. By default, all physics objects are set to collision group 0. This means that they will not collide with other objects without a specific collision event. Assigning a positive number to this setting will cause the object in question to collide with all other objects in the same collision group, regardless of collision events. Assigning a negative number will prevent the object from colliding with any objects in that group. I don't recommend that you use collision groups unless absolutely necessary, as it takes a great deal of memory to work properly.

- **Linear damping**: Linear damping works a lot like air friction in real life. This setting affects the velocity (momentum) of objects in motion over time. Imagine a military shooter where thrown grenades don't arc, they just keep soaring through the air. We don't need this. That's what rockets are for.

- **Angular damping**: Angular damping is similar to linear damping. It only affects an object's rotation. This setting keeps objects from spinning forever. Have you ever ridden the Teacup ride at Disneyland? If so, you will know that angular damping is a good thing.

- **Friction**: Friction also works in a similar way to linear damping, but it affects an object's momentum as it collides with another object or surface. If you want to create icy surfaces in a platformer, friction is your friend.

We didn't use this menu in this recipe but we did set and modify these settings through code. First, in each of the objects, we set them to use physics and then declared their shapes and collision masks. We started with declaring the `fixture` variable because, as you can see, it is part of each of the functions we used and typing `fixture` is easier than typing `physics_fixture_create()` every time. The `fixture` variable that we bind to the object is what is actually being affected by forces and other physics objects, so we must set its shape and properties in order to tell GameMaker how it should react. In order to set the fixture's shape, we use `physics_set_circle_shape`, `physics_set_box_shape`, and `physics_set_polygon_shape`. These functions define the collision mask associated with the object in question. In the case of the circle, we got the radius from half the width of the sprite, whereas for the box, we found the outer edges used via half the width and half the height. GameMaker then uses this information to create a collision mask to match the sprite from which the information was gathered. When creating a fixture from a more complex sprite, you can either use the aforementioned methods to approximate a mask, or you can create a more complex shape using a polygon like we did for the triangle. You'll notice that the code to create the triangle fixture had extra lines. This is because polygons require you to map each point on the shape you're trying to create. You can map three to eight points by telling GameMaker where each one is situated in relation to the center of the image (0, 0). One very important detail is that you cannot create a concave shape; this will result in an error.

Every fixture you create must have a convex shape. The only way to create a concave fixture is to actually create multiple fixtures in the same object. If you were to take the code for the triangle, duplicate all of it in the same code block and alter the coordinates for each point in the duplicated code; you can create concave shapes. For example, you can use two rectangles to make an *L* shape. This can only be done using a polygon fixture, as it is the only fixture that allows you to code the position of individual points.

Once you've coded the shape of your fixture, you can begin to code its attributes. I've described what each physics option does, and you've coded and tested them using the instructions mentioned earlier. Now, take a look at the values for each setting. The ball object has a higher restitution than the rest; did you notice how it bounced? The box object has a very low friction; it slides around on platforms as though it is made of ice. The triangle has very low density and angular damping; it is easily knocked around by the other objects and spins like crazy. You can change how objects react to forces and collisions by changing one or more of these values. I definitely recommend that you play around with these settings to see what you can come up with.

Remember how the ground objects are static? Notice how we still had to code them? Well, that's because they still interact with other objects but in an almost opposite fashion. Since we set the object's density to 0, GameMaker more or less views this as an object that is infinitely dense; it cannot be moved by outside forces or collisions. It can, however, affect other objects. We don't have to set the angular and linear damping values simply because the ground doesn't move. We do, however, have to set the restitution and friction levels because we need to tell GameMaker how other objects should react when they come in contact with the ground. Do you want to make a rubber wall to bounce a player off? Set the restitution to a higher level. Do you want to make that icy patch we talked about? Then, you need to lower the friction. These are some fun settings to play around with, so try it out.

Alternating gravity

Gravity can be a harsh mistress; if you've ever fallen from a height, you know what I mean. I often think it would be great if we could somehow lessen gravity's hold on us, but then I wonder what it would be like if we could just reverse it all together! Imagine flipping a switch and then walking on the ceiling! I, for one, think that it would be great. However, since we don't have the technology to do it in real life, I'll have to settle for doing it in video games.

Getting ready

For this recipe, let's simplify things and use the physics environment that we created in the previous recipe.

How to do it

1. In `obj_control`, open the code block in the **Create** event.
2. Add the following code:

```
physics_world_gravity(0, -10);
```

That's it! Test the environment and see what happens when you create your physics objects.

How it works

GameMaker's physics world gravity is vector-based. This means that you simply need to change the values of *x* and *y* in order to change how gravity works in a particular room. If you take a look at the **Physics** tab in the room editor, you'll see that there are values under *x* and *y*. The default value is 0 for *x* and 10 for *y*. When we added this code to the control object's **Create** event, we changed the value of *y* to -10, which means that it will flow in the opposite direction. You can change the direction to 360 degrees by altering both *x* and *y*, and you can change the gravity's strength by raising and lowering the values.

There's more

Alternating gravity's flow can be a lot of fun in a platformer. Several games have explored this in different ways. Your character can change gravity by hitting a switch in a game, the player can change it by pressing a button, or you can just give specific areas different gravity settings. Play around with this and see what you can create.

Applying force via magnets

Remember playing with magnets in science class when you were a kid? It was fun back then, right? Well, it's still fun; powerful magnets make a great gift for your favorite office worker. What about virtual magnets, though? Are they still fun? The answer is yes. Yes, they are.

Getting ready

Once again, we're simply going to modify our existing physics environment in order to add some new functionalities.

How to do it

1. In `obj_control`, open the code block in the **Step** event.

2. Add the following code:

```
if keyboard_check(vk_space)
{
with (obj_dynamicParent)
    {
    var dir = point_direction(x,y,mouse_x,mouse_y);
    physics_apply_force(x, y, lengthdir_x(30, dir),
lengthdir_y(30, dir));
    }
}
```

Once you close the code block, you can test your new magnet. Add some objects, hold down the spacebar, and see what happens.

How it works

Applying a force to a physics-enabled object in GameMaker will add a given value to the direction, rotation, and speed of said object. Force can be used to gradually propel an object in a given direction, or through a little math, as in this case, draw objects nearer. What we're doing here is while the Spacebar is held down, any objects in the vicinity are drawn to the magnet (in this case, your mouse). In order to accomplish this, we first declare that the following code needs to act on `obj_dynamicParent`, as opposed to acting on the control object where the code resides. We then set the value of a `dir` variable to the `point_ direction` of the mouse, as it relates to any child of `obj_dynamicParent`. From there, we can begin to apply force. With `physics_apply_force`, the first two values represent the *x* and *y* coordinates of the object to which the force is being applied. Since the object(s) in question is/are not static, we simply set the coordinates to whatever value they have at the time. The other two values are used in tandem to calculate the direction in which the object will travel and the force propelling it in Newtons. We get these values, in this instance, by calculating the `lengthdir` for both *x* and *y*. The `lengthdir` finds the *x* or *y* value of a point at a given length (we used 30) at a given angle (we used `dir`, which represents `point_ direction`, that finds the angle where the mouse's coordinates lie). If you want to increase the length value, then you need to increase the power of the magnet.

Creating a moving platform

We've now seen both static and dynamic physics objects in GameMaker, but what happens when we want the best of both worlds? Let's take a look at how to create a platform that can move and affect other objects via collisions but is immune to said collisions.

Getting ready

Again, we'll be using our existing physics environment, but this time, we'll need a new object. Create a sprite that is 128 px wide by 32 px high and assign it to an object called `obj_platform`. Also, create another object called `obj_kinematicParent` but don't give it a sprite. Add collision events to `obj_staticParent`, `obj_dynamicParent`, and itself. Make sure that there is a comment in each event.

How to do it

1. In `obj_platform`, add a **Create** event.

2. Drag a code block to the **Actions** box and add the following code:
   ```
   var fixture = physics_fixture_create();
   physics_fixture_set_box_shape(fixture, sprite_width / 2, sprite_height / 2);
   physics_fixture_set_density(fixture, 0);
   physics_fixture_set_restitution(fixture, 0.2);
   physics_fixture_set_friction(fixture, 0.5);
   physics_fixture_bind(fixture, id);
   physics_fixture_delete(fixture);
   phy_speed_x = 5;
   ```

3. Add a **Step** event with a code block containing the following code:
   ```
   if (x <64) or (x > room_width-64)
   {
       phy_speed_x = phy_speed_x * -1;
   }
   ```

4. Place an instance of `obj_platform` in the room, which is slightly higher than the highest instance of `obj_ground`.

Once this is done, you can go ahead and test it. Try dropping various objects on the platform and see what happens!

How it works

Kinematic objects in GameMaker's physics world are essentially static objects that can move. While the platform has a density of 0, it also has a speed of 5 along the x axis. You'll notice that we didn't just use speed = 5, as this would not have the desired effect in a physics world. The code in the steps simply causes the platform to remain within a set boundary by multiplying its current horizontal speed by -1. Any static object to which movement is applied automatically becomes a kinematic object.

Making a rope

Is there anything more useful than a rope? I mean besides your computer, your phone or even this book. Probably a lot of things, but that doesn't make a rope any less useful. Ropes and chains are also useful in games. Some games, such as *Cut the Rope*, have based their entire gameplay structure around them. Let's see how we can create ropes and chains in GameMaker.

Getting ready

For this recipe, you can either continue using the physics environment that we've been working with, or you can simply start from scratch. If you've gone through the rest of this chapter, you should be fairly comfortable with setting up physics objects. I completed this recipe with a fresh .gmx file.

Before we begin, go ahead and set up obj_dynamicParent and obj_staticParent with collision events for one another. Next, you'll need to create the obj_ropeHome, obj_rope, obj_block, and obj_ropeControl objects. The sprite for obj_rope can simply be a 4 px wide by 16 px high box, while obj_ropeHome and obj_block can be 32 px squares. Obj_ropeControl needs to use the same sprite as obj_rope, but with the y origin set to 0. Obj_ropeControl should also be invisible.

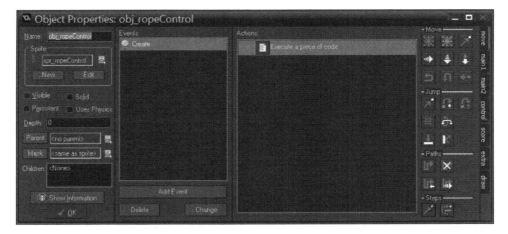

As for parenting, `obj_rope` should be a child of `obj_dynamicParent` and `obj_ropeHome`, and `obj_block` should be children of `obj_staticParent`, and `obj_ropeControl` does not require any parent at all. As always, you'll also need a room in which to place your objects.

How to do it

1. Open `obj_ropeHome` and add a **Create** event.

2. Place a code block in the **Actions** box and add the following code:

    ```
    var fixture = physics_fixture_create();
    physics_fixture_set_box_shape(fixture, sprite_width / 2, sprite_
    height / 2); physics_fixture_set_density(fixture, 0);
    physics_fixture_set_restitution(fixture, 0.2);
    physics_fixture_set_friction(fixture, 0.5);
    physics_fixture_bind(fixture, id);
    physics_fixture_delete(fixture);
    ```

3. In `obj_rope`, add a **Create** event with a code block.

4. Enter the following code:

    ```
    var fixture = physics_fixture_create();
    physics_fixture_set_box_shape(fixture, sprite_width / 2, sprite_
    height / 2);
    physics_fixture_set_density(fixture, 0.25);
    physics_fixture_set_restitution(fixture, 0.01);
    physics_fixture_set_linear_damping(fixture, 0.5);
    physics_fixture_set_angular_damping(fixture, 1);
    physics_fixture_set_friction(fixture, 0.5);
    physics_fixture_bind(fixture, id);
    physics_fixture_delete(fixture);
    ```

5. Open `obj_ropeControl` and add a **Create** event.

6. Drag a code block to the **Actions** box and enter the following code:

    ```
    setLength = image_yscale-1;
    ropeLength = 16;
    rope1 = instance_create(x,y,obj_ropeHome2);
    rope2 = instance_create(x,y,obj_rope2);
    physics_joint_revolute_create(rope1, rope2, rope1.x, rope1.y,
    0,0,0,0,0,0,0);
    repeat (setLength)
    {
    ```

```
        ropeLength += 16;
        rope1 = rope2;
        rope2 = instance_create(x, y+ropeLength, obj_rope2);
        physics_joint_revolute_create(rope1, rope2, rope1.x, rope1.y,
0,0,0,0,0,0,0);
    }
```

7. In obj_block, add a **Create** event.

8. Place a code block in the **Actions** box and add the following code:

```
var fixture = physics_fixture_create();
physics_fixture_set_circle_shape(fixture, sprite_get_width(spr_
ropeHome)/2);
physics_fixture_set_density(fixture, 0);
physics_fixture_set_restitution(fixture, 0.01);
physics_fixture_set_friction(fixture, 0.5);
physics_fixture_bind(fixture, id);
physics_fixture_delete(fixture);
```

9. Now, add a **Step** event with the following code in a code block:

```
phy_position_x = mouse_x;
phy_position_y = mouse_y;
```

10. Place an instance of obj_ropeControl anywhere in the room. This will be the starting point of the rope. You can place multiple instances of the object if you wish.

11. For every instance of obj_ropeControl you place in the room, use the bounding box to stretch it to however long you wish. This will determine the length of your rope.

12. Place a single instance of obj_block in the room.

Once you've completed these steps, you can go ahead and test them.

How it works

This recipe may seem somewhat complicated but it's really not. What you're doing here is taking multiple instances of the same physics-enabled object and stringing them together. Since you're using instances of the same object, you only have to code one and the rest will follow.

Once again, our collisions are handled by our parent objects. This way, you don't have to set collisions for each object. Also, setting the physical properties of each object is done exactly as we have done in previous recipes. By setting the density of obj_ropeHome and obj_block to 0, we're ensuring that they are not affected by gravity or collisions, but they can still collide with other objects and affect them. In this case, we set the physics coordinates of obj_block to those of the mouse so that, when testing, you can use them to collide with the rope, moving it.

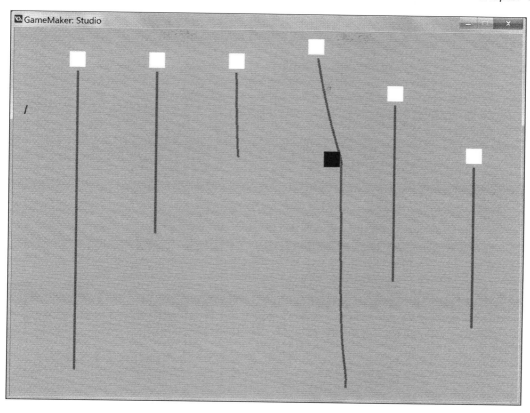

The most complex code takes place in the **Create** event for obj_ropeControl. Here, we not only define how many sections of a rope or chain will be used, but we also define how they are connected. To begin, the *y* scale of the control object is measured in order to determine how many instances of obj_rope are required. Based on how long you stretched obj_ropeControl in the room, the rope will be longer (more instances) or shorter (fewer instances). We then set a variable (ropeLength) to the size of the sprite used for obj_rope. This will be used later to tell GameMaker where each instance of obj_rope should be so that we can connect them in a line. Next, we create the object that will hold the obj_ropeHome rope. This is a static object that will not move, no matter how much the rope moves. This is connected to the first instance of obj_rope via a revolute joint. In GameMaker, a revolute joint is used in several ways: it can act as part of a motor, moving pistons; it can act as a joint on a ragdoll body; in this case, it acts as the connection between instances of obj_rope. A revolute joint allows the programmer to code its angle and torque, but for our purposes, this isn't necessary. We declared the objects that are connected via the joint as well as the anchor location, but the other values remain null. Once the rope holder (obj_ropeHome) and initial joint are set up, we can automate the creation of the rest. Using the repeat function, we can tell GameMaker to repeat a block of code a set number of times.

In this case, this number is derived from how many instances of `obj_rope` can fit within the distance between the *y* origin of `obj_ropeControl` and the point to which you stretched it. We subtract 1 from this number as GameMaker will calculate too many in order to cover the distance in its entirety. The code that will be repeated does a few things at once. First, it increases the value of the `ropeLength` variable by 16 for each instance that is calculated. Then, GameMaker changes the value of `rope1` (which creates an instance of `obj_ropeHome`) to that of `rope2` (which creates an instance of `obj_rope`). The `rope2` variable is then reestablished to create an instance of `obj_rope`, but also adds the new value of `ropeLength` so as to move its coordinates directly below those of the previous instance, thus creating a chain. This process is repeated until the set length of the overall rope is reached.

There's more

Each section of rope is a physics object and acts as such in the physics world. By changing the physics settings when initially creating the rope sections, you can see how they react to collisions. How far and how quickly the rope moves when pushed by another object is very much related to the difference between their densities. If you make the rope denser than the object colliding with it, the rope will move very little. If you reverse these values, you can cause the rope to flail about, wildly. Play around with the settings and see what happens, but when placing a rope or chain in a game, you really must consider what the rope and other objects are made of. It wouldn't seem right for a lead chain to be sent flailing about by a collision with a pillow, now would it?

5
Now Hear This! – Music and Sound Effects

In this chapter, we'll cover the following topics:

- ▶ Importing and playing background music
- ▶ Implementing situational sound effects
- ▶ Adding sound emitters and listeners
- ▶ Adjusting the listener orientation
- ▶ Replicating the Doppler effect with emitters

Introduction

When you think about it, sound is not absolutely necessary to the majority of video games; most of us have played a game with the sound off at one point or another. Having said this, most gamers would certainly agree that sound effects and music make the experience much more enjoyable. In fact, there are many games in which sound and music comprise most, if not all, of the gameplay. Consider playing *Guitar Hero* or *Rock Band* with no sound. While you could play and win based solely on the visual cues, why would you want to? The fun of rhythm and music games lies in the rhythm and music. Take the music out of *Dance Dance Revolution* and you're just stomping on a beat pad.

A game's music and effects definitely add to the experience and are often part of our gaming memories. When I think of my favorite games, I can always remember the music that played in the background and the sound effects as I played. While this is true for most gamers, the opposite effect can be said about music and sounds that just don't fit. If your character is shooting a gun but it sounds like a barking dog, it's really hard to lose yourself in the game's world.

Getting a game's sound just right can be difficult, but with the right know-how you can at least get started. Let's take a look at GameMaker's sound system and what it can do for you.

Audio basics

The first step to implementing audio in GameMaker is to learn the basics. We'll take a look at some core elements of importing and playing audio:

- ▶ Importing and playing background music

Sound effects

Sound effects can add so much to a game to make it more engaging and interesting. It would seem weird if your character collected a coin and there was no "ba-ding!" right? Let's add some sound effects to our gameplay:

- ▶ Implementing situational sound effects

3D audio

Sometimes having simple sound effects just isn't enough. GameMaker's sound system allows you to simulate 3D space using audio:

- ▶ Adding sound emitters and listeners
- ▶ Adjusting listener orientation
- ▶ Replicating the Doppler effect with moving emitters

Importing and playing background music

Personally, I feel that music affects my enjoyment of a game in a big way. I have my favorite game music such as the level two background music from *Super Mario Bros. 3*, the *Song of Storms from Legend of Zelda: Ocarina of Time*, and the entire soundtrack of *Capy Games' Superbrothers: Sword & Sworcery*. They each bring with them a certain element of nostalgia, as they play an important role in my gaming history. It's tough to say, with certainty, whether my enjoyment of each of these games could have been affected by a change in the music, but I think it could. I'm sure if you think of your favorite moments from your favorite games, you can hear the music in your head. Keeping this in mind (no pun intended), let's learn a little about importing and playing music in GameMaker.

Getting ready

You'll need three things to begin this recipe: a room (of course), an object called `obj_musicControl`, and a song of your choice. You can use either an `.mp3` or a `.wav`; I chose the former. Once you have these elements, you're ready to begin.

How to do it

1. Click on the **Create a sound** button on your toolbar. It's the one that looks like a small speaker when viewed from the front. The following menu will pop up:

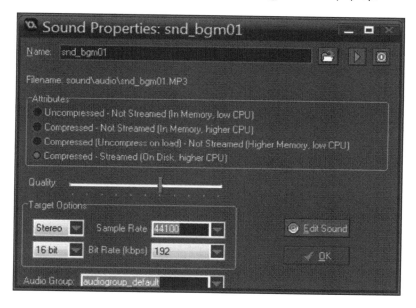

2. Click on the **Load sound from a file** button (the folder icon) and select your music file.
3. Name your sound for use in GameMaker. I chose `snd_bgm01`.
4. Under **Attributes**, select **Compressed—Streamed** and click on **Ok**.
5. In `obj_musicControl`, add a **Create** event.
6. Drag a code block to the **Actions** box and enter the following code:

```
audio_play_sound(snd_bgm01, 1, true);
pause = false;
stop = false;
state = "Play";
```

7. Add a **Step** event to a code block containing the following code:

```
if keyboard_check_pressed(ord('P'))
{
    pause = !pause;
    if pause
    {
        audio_pause_sound(snd_bgm01);
        state = "Pause";
    }
    else
    {
        audio_resume_sound(snd_bgm01);
        state = "Play";
    }
}
if keyboard_check_pressed(ord('S'))
{
    stop = !stop;
    if stop
    {
        audio_stop_sound(snd_bgm01);
        state = "Stop";
    }
    else
    {
        audio_play_sound(snd_bgm01, 1, true);
        state = "Play";
    }
}
```

8. Add a **Draw** event and place a code block in the **Actions** box.

9. Enter the following code:

```
draw_text(room_width/2,320,string(state));
```

Once this is complete, you can add your music controller object to the room and test it. Use the *S* and *P* keys on your keyboard to pause, stop, and play your music, which should play right from the get-go.

How it works

This recipe is quite simple and is really just used to demonstrate a few basics of sound in GameMaker. Importing sound files work in the same way, whether it is music or sound effects. You can import either an .mp3 or a .wav from the **Sound Properties** editor and the settings can be changed at any time. One very important thing you need to remember is that when you rename a sound file, you need to change any instance that appears in code. Similarly, if you change the sound you associate with a particular name, you'll need to remember where you used it in the code; otherwise, you could end up with a sound playing at an undesired moment. Once you've given your sound a proper name, preferably following an appropriate naming convention, you're ready to call instances of the sound in the game.

In the **Sound Properties** editor, you'll notice a few things. The first is the selection for audio compression and playback, which are very important things to consider. Your options come in the form of whether the sound is compressed and whether it is streamed. In order to make the right choice, you really need to take a look at what you're uploading (sound effect or music) and how memory and CPU intensive your game will be. In our case, we uploaded some background music. For this reason, we chose to use an .mp3 file (a smaller file size) and we selected **Compressed—Streamed**. This means that the file size is further compressed (saves disc space when packaging your game) and is unloaded as the .mp3 file is played. This requires more work from the CPU but because the file is loaded in smaller chunks, it is ideal for music files. This would not be ideal for sound effects (which are usually much shorter but played more frequently), just as you would not want to have a song file uncompressed in its entirety every time it is played.

If you choose an .mp3 sound file, you'll notice a quality meter that allows you to adjust the sound quality, and thus memory and CPU requirements for this particular file. Below this, you'll see the **Target** options. This is where you can adjust whether the file should be played as mono, stereo, or 3D audio, as well as the sample and bit rates. You can also edit the file itself as long as you've associated an audio editing program, as GameMaker does not have a built-in editor.

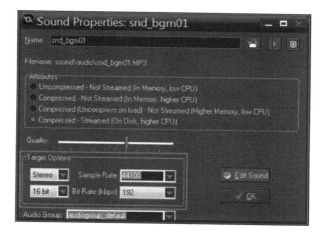

With the file loaded and selections made, your background music is ready to go. What we've done in this recipe is simply have the song begin to play when the music control object loads using the `audio_play_sound` function. This function will be used to play all sounds and music by calling an instance of the sound (which acts like an object at this point), assigning a channel priority, and indicating whether it will be looped or not. The instance's priority will be used to manage which sounds will be stopped and which will continue to play in the event where too many sound files are playing at once or taking up too much memory. You can assign priority with numbers from 0 to 1 or 0 to 100. In our case, the priority isn't important (as we have only one sound file playing) but we did make it loop. The rest of the recipe demonstrates `audio_pause_sound`, `audio_resume_sound`, and `audio_stop_sound`, all of which are used exactly as their names suggest.

There's more

There are several other basic functions used for GameMaker's audio system. You can use `audio_exists` to verify that a particular sound file is packaged and `audio_get_name` to identify an audio file's name (which is good for music menus and displaying a song title as it plays). You can also use `audio_is_playing` or `audio_is_paused` to verify the play state of a particular sound instance and `audio_pause_all` and `audio_stop_all` to halt the play of any sounds (both music and sound effects) that may be playing at the time.

Implementing situational sound effects

Ever noticed how almost anything that you do in games produces some kind of sound effect? It could be as simple as a "ding!" every time you collect gold or a complex series of explosions coming from your speakers, but in the best games, a lot of thought and planning goes into sound design because it is really important to the experience. Sound in games, at its core, is meant to inform the player of something happening. If the sound doesn't match the action, it can break a player's engagement with the game world. You've likely played a game with poor sound design; you might not remember it, but you surely remember the games that did it right. Let's take a look at how we can create audible responses to accompany in-game events.

Getting ready

For this recipe, we're going to reuse some of the movement code from *Chapter 2, It's Under Control – Exploring Various Control Schemes.* If you skipped the *Making your character jump* recipe; don't worry, I've copied everything you need here. What you *will* need, however, is a player character and platform on which this character can jump. The first object you'll need should be called `obj_ground_parent` and requires no sprite. The second object should be called `obj_ground` requires a sprite (this should just be a colored square) and needs `obj_ground_parent` set as the parent object. Lastly, you'll need `obj_player` with the sprite of your choice. In a room, create a small platform using instances of `obj_ground` and place an instance of `obj_player` on top.

How to do it

1. In `obj_player`, add a **Create** event.
2. Drag a code block to the **Actions** box and enter the following code:

```
soundState = 0;
grav = 1;
grav_max = 10;
```

3. Add a **Step** event and place a code block in the **Actions** box.
4. In the code block, enter the following code:

```
if (!place_meeting(x, y+(vspeed/2), obj_ground_parent))
{
    if vspeed < grav_max
    {
        vspeed+=grav;
    }
}
else
{
    vspeed = 0;
}
if keyboard_check_pressed(vk_space) and (place_meeting(x,
y+vspeed, obj_ground_parent))
{
    jump_spd = ((soundState + 1) * 7);
    vspeed = -jump_spd;
    var jump = audio_play_sound(snd_sfx_jump, 5, false);
    if soundState = 0
    {
        audio_sound_pitch(jump, 1.3);
    }
    if soundState = 1
    {
        audio_sound_pitch(jump, 1);
    }
    if soundState = 2
    {
        audio_sound_pitch(jump, 0.7);
    }
    soundState += 1;
    if soundState > 2
    {
```

```
                        soundState = 0;
            }
    }
}
```

You can now close the **Object Properties** editor for `obj_player` and test the program. Use the Spacebar to jump and see what happens. Make sure your speakers are turned on!

How it works

In this recipe, we simply want to have a sound play when the player character jumps. What I've shown you, however, is a method of altering the way in which a sound is played back in GameMaker. Did you notice that the sound changed to match the height to which the player jumped? This is to show that sound plays an important role in the overall game experience. We controlled this using `audio_sound_pitch` to alter the pitch of the sound we played without having a separate file. Do you want to see just how much sound matters? Try reversing the values in each jump. Set the first jump to a pitch of `0.7` and the third jump to a pitch of `1.3` and test it out. It doesn't fit nearly as well, does it?

Essentially, `audio_sound_pitch` does exactly what it says it does; it sets a sound's pitch. In order to use it, you'll need to set a variable to contain the `audio_play_sound` function in order to have a pitch to be set in the first place. Try playing around with the pitch by changing the number used. Keep in mind that it *is* possible to go too far here; a pitch value below 0 or over 5 will produce a sound that is unlikely to be audible. Well, audible to humans, at least; you never know what your dog might think of it.

There's more

The method that we used earlier for selecting a pitch based on the `soundState` value has only one method for such a task. When selecting an outcome based on the value of a variable, you can also use the switch function. To get the same results with fewer lines of code, replace this:

```
if soundState = 0
{
    audio_sound_pitch(jump, 1.3);
}
if soundState = 1
{
    audio_sound_pitch(jump, 1);
}
if soundState = 2
{
    audio_sound_pitch(jump, 0.7);
}
```

With this:

```
switch (soundState)
{
    case 0: audio_sound_pitch(jump, 1.3);
    break;
    case 1: audio_sound_pitch(jump, 1);
    break;
    case 2: audio_sound_pitch(jump, 0.7);
    break;
}
```

GameMaker is given instructions for each state the same as the previous method, but in a cleaner, easier-to-read way. GameMaker will search the list of cases until it finds the appropriate one and then it will run it. Keep in mind that you need to use `break` after each case to prevent GameMaker from continuing to run each subsequent case instead of ending where appropriate.

Adding sound emitters and listeners

With its updated audio engine, GameMaker has added the ability to simulate 3D sound. This doesn't mean that you have to make a 3D game to utilize it, however; you can use this feature to add depth (figurative and literal) to your 2D world. Let's take a look at some basics for creating location-dependent audio.

Getting ready

This recipe calls one sound file (I used a 13-second loop of rushing water; it is a public domain sound I downloaded from `http://soundbible.com/`): a player object (our listener) and emitter object. Give the player and the emitter their own sprites. Though a sprite for the latter isn't necessary, we're going to make it visible so that you have a point of reference when you test it. We'll call the emitter, `obj_water`, and our player character something crazy such as `obj_player`. Create a room and place both the objects in it with `obj_water` near the center.

How to do it

1. Click on the **Create** a sound icon and load your audio.
2. Call the sound object, `snd_sfx_water`, and set the compression to **Compressed** (uncompress on load).
3. Under the **Target** options, set the audio to 3D (default is mono) and close the editor.

4. In `obj_player`, add a **Create** event and drag a code block to the **Actions** box.

5. Enter the following code:

   ```
   audio_listener_orientation(0, 1, 0, 0, 0, 1);
   ```

6. Add a **Step** event.

7. Place a code block with the following code:

   ```
   if keyboard_check(vk_left)
   {
       x -= 5;
   }
   if keyboard_check(vk_right)
   {
       x += 5;
   }
   if keyboard_check(vk_up)
   {
       y -= 5;
   }
   if keyboard_check(vk_down)
   {
       y += 5;
   }
   audio_listener_position(x, y, 0);
   ```

8. In `obj_water`, add a **Create** event.

9. In a code block, enter this code:

   ```
   snd_emit = audio_emitter_create();
   audio_emitter_position(snd_emit, x, y, 0);
   audio_falloff_set_model(audio_falloff_linear_distance);
   audio_emitter_falloff(snd_emit, 100, 300, 1);
   audio_play_sound_on(snd_emit, snd_sfx_water, true, 1);
   ```

10. Add a **Room End** event (found in the **Other event category**).

11. Place a code block in the **Actions** box with the following code:

    ```
    sound_stop(snd_sfx_water);
    ```

Once this is complete, you can test your scene. Use the arrow keys to move your player around the room. The audio should change depending on where you are in relation to the emitter, in terms of both distance and position.

How it works

Emitters and listeners allow you to easily create some great scenes. Through the use of audio falloff and listener orientation, GameMaker can add a great deal of realism and polish to any project.

What we've done here is we've created an audio listener that follows the player's position. GameMaker takes this position in relation to any emitters in the room and alters the gain of the audio associated with each emitter. We created an audio emitter, and using `audio_emitter_position`, we can tell GameMaker where this emitter is situated in the room. We then used `audio_falloff_set_model` to dictate how falloff works for that particular sound and `audio_emitter_falloff` to set where falloff begins and how far the sound should reach, in terms of the emitter's position. Try playing around with the values used for the falloff reference, maximum falloff, and falloff factor. These values will alter how and where the audio will be heard by the listener. Finally, `audio_play_sound_on` assigns a sound object to the emitter, tells it whether to loop or not, and sets the sound's priority. As we're only using one sound here, the value used to set priority is essentially inconsequential.

One last, but very important, thing is to stop the emitter from playing a sound when it is no longer needed. In our case, we set the sound file to stop playing when we exit the room. If you attach the emitter to an enemy, you can also accomplish this when the enemy instance is destroyed. If the emitter no longer serves a purpose, it is highly recommended that you get rid of it. This is because the emitter will keep emitting until it is told not to. If left alone, this can result in high CPU usage or memory leaks and can cause your game to crash. Keep your emitters in check!

There's more

In this recipe, we used a linear falloff model. This allows the emitter to set the audio's gain to 0, but sacrifices a more gradual falloff. If you use `audio_falloff_exponent_distance` or `audio_falloff_inverse_distance`, you can get a much smoother and more gradual falloff, but the audio will keep growing quieter without actually becoming inaudible.

Adjusting the listener orientation

Let's say you're making a top-down shooter and you want the player to really get into the role of the characters they're controlling. You would want them to experience the environment in the same way and this includes the sounds he/she will hear. Since we already have our emitter and listener, let's take a look at how we can affect the audio based on the orientation of the player (the listener).

Getting ready

You can use the code and setup from the previous recipe; we're just going to adjust some of the code here and there.

How to do it

1. Open `obj_player` and delete the **Create** event.

2. In the **Step** event, add the following code to the bottom of your code block:

```
image_angle = point_direction(x, y, mouse_x, mouse_y);
audio_listener_orientation(lengthdir_x(1, image_angle),
lengthdir_y(1, image_angle), 5, 0, 0, -1);
```

Once this is done you can test the new code. Move the player around the room but move the mouse as well. The player will rotate around based on the mouse's position, but you'll notice that the audio is affected as well.

Once again, I used a public domain sound from `http://soundbible.com/`. Use your sound to create a sound in GameMaker with the same settings as the water effect in the previous recipe.

How it works

All we've done here is set the listener's orientation to match the direction in which the player is facing. If the emitter is adjacent to the player's right ear, the audio will come out of the right speaker and vice versa. Now, we need to make a note of a few things. Firstly, when using 3D audio such as this, you must account for the *z* vector. Here, we've set the listener to sit at a *z* look vector of 5, and we've pointed it to face up by setting the *z* up vector to -1. This ensures that the player character is oriented appropriately to receive the audio information. Had we set the z up vector to 1, the speakers would be reversed, as the player would be flipped. We've also used `lenghtdir_x` and `lengthdir_y` to set the *x* and *y* look vectors to match the location of the mouse. This way, the listener always faces the direction of the mouse, just like the sprite. As a result, we get audio that matches our visuals.

Replicating the Doppler effect with emitters

If you've ever stood by the side of a road as cars pass by, you've experienced the Doppler effect. Without getting into too much detail, the Doppler effect is the change in frequency of a wave (in this case, a sound wave) for an observer moving relative to its source. In the case of a car moving by a stationary observer (that is, you), the sound waves caused by the car's engine are being emitted closer together as the car approaches than they are as the car recedes. That's why a car emits a higher pitch noise the closer it gets and a lower pitch noise as it passes by and drives away. With the help of GameMaker's 3D audio functions, we can actually recreate this effect.

Getting ready

Once again, we'll be using the player object that we created in the *Adding sound emitters and listeners* recipe. Make sure that the **Create** event for obj_player contains the following code:

```
audio_listener_orientation(0, 1, 0, 0, 0, 1);
```

Make sure that the **Step** event *does not* contain the mouse-based orientation code, as we will not be using it here. We will, however, need to keep the audio_listener_position line of code. Also, remove the emitter object (obj_water) that we placed in the room, as we'll be creating a new one.

Once this is done, create an object (with a sprite) called obj_car. You'll also need a sound file of a car driving. Try not to use the sound of a car passing by, as this is the effect we're trying to reproduce.

How to do it

1. In obj_player, add a **Create** event.
2. Drag a code block to the **Actions** box and add the following code:
   ```
   hspeed = global.carSpeed;
   snd_emitCar = audio_emitter_create();
   audio_falloff_set_model(audio_falloff_exponent_distance);
   audio_emitter_falloff(snd_emitCar, 25, 200, 1.5);
   audio_play_sound_on(snd_emitCar, snd_sfx_car, true, 1);
   ```
3. Add a **Step** event and place a code block in the **Actions** box.
4. Enter the following code:
   ```
   audio_emitter_position(snd_emitCar, x, y, 0);
   audio_emitter_velocity(snd_emitCar, hspeed, vspeed, 0);
   ```
5. Add an **Outside Room** event, which is under the **Other** events.
6. Place a code block and enter the following code:
   ```
   if global.carSpeed < 50
   {
       global.carSpeed = (global.carSpeed * 1.2);
   }
   sound_stop(snd_sfx_car);
   instance_create(0, room_height/2, obj_car);
   instance_destroy();
   ```

Once these steps are complete, place an instance of `obj_car` in the room on the left-hand side about half way down. It doesn't have to be exact as it will correct itself on the second pass anyway. You are now ready to test it. Move your player around to see the effects from different positions and try playing with the falloff settings to see further changes.

How it works

This code works just as you would expect. The `audio_emitter_velocity` function simulates how your selected audio file would sound if it were to move at your selected speed. There are four values to set when using this function: the sound file to be played and the *x*, *y*, and *z* velocities in pixels per step. Here, we've set the *x* and *y* velocities to be set by the car object's speed. Since this is a 2D test, there is no movement on the *z* axis, and therefore, there's no need for a *z* velocity value. By telling GameMaker to set the sound emitter's velocity to be that of the car object, the sound is altered whenever the car changes speed. Without `audio_emitter_velocity`, you wouldn't get the same effect; you could make the emitter move with the car object, but the audio wouldn't change. One thing to keep in mind is that it *is* possible for the emitter to go too fast. You'll notice that we've capped the car's speed at 50. This is because once the car's velocity gets too high, the audio becomes unintelligible. If you're using this function for an object that moves at a constant speed (say, a bullet), you can set the velocity variables as constants. It's always a good idea to play around with the values until it sounds right.

6
It's All GUI! - Creating Graphical User Interface and Menus

In this chapter, we'll cover the following topics:

- ▸ Setting up a basic HUD with code
- ▸ Making your HUD scalable
- ▸ Using the GUI layer in full screen mode with views
- ▸ Adding a title screen
- ▸ Creating splash pages
- ▸ Adding a game over screen

Introduction

Of all the game terms that are fun to say, GUI (often pronounced "gooey") is probably the most important. **Graphical User Interface (GUI)** refers to any on-screen visual cues that allow the user to control the software directly. This is usually associated with images and texts that provide information and points of interaction, such as menus and icons.

GUIs are most commonly associated with software applications, as opposed to video games. While video games are a form of software, many prefer this differentiation. In video games, a more common term for display and menu items would be **HUD** (also fun to say), which stands for **Heads-Up Display**. While these two terms mean largely the same thing, HUD is viewed by most as the preferred term. Having said this, GameMaker uses GUI to describe such systems, so we'll stick to this. With these formalities out of the way, let's take a look at how GameMaker handles menus, game screens, and the GUI in general.

GUI basics

In *Chapter 1, Game Plan – Creating Basic Gameplay,* we made a basic GUI using GameMaker's drag and drop interface. This works just fine but, by coding it yourself, you can fine-tune this interface to your needs.

- Setting up a basic HUD with code
- Making your HUD scalable
- Using the GUI layer in full screen mode

Game screens and menus

Having a game that starts as soon as you open it is fine for testing or for a proof of concept but it's not ideal for making an actual game product. We'll take a look at how we can implement various game screens:

- Adding a title screen
- Creating splash pages
- Adding a "Game Over" screen

Setting up a basic HUD with code

Have you ever played a game and stopped to think, "Gee, I wish I knew what my score was!" No? That's probably because your score, health, and other important pieces of information are presented to you on the screen at any given moment. Now, this isn't the case for *all* games; of course, but it's true for classic and arcade games. *Pac-Man* and *Mario* will always tell you how many lives you have left with because it's important to have this information. Let's take a look at how we can display such information by making a simple game.

Getting ready

You'll need a few things before we can really begin. Firstly, you'll need to create a room called `rm_game`. You'll also need four objects: `obj_display`, `obj_gameControl`, `obj_base`, and `obj_enemy`. The last two will require sprites. You'll also need to set up a new font. This does not need to be a custom font designed by you. Simply, click on the **Create a font** button on the toolbar, select the font you wish to use to display health, lives, and scores, and customize the style and size.

Name the font `fnt_HUD` in order to reference it in your code. Once this is complete, you're ready to go.

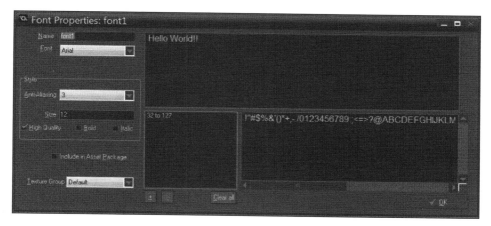

How to do it

1. Open `obj_display` and add a **Create** event.

2. Drag a code block to the **Actions** box and enter the following code:

```
global.playerHealth = 100;
global.playerLives = 3;
global.playerScore = 0;
global.gameOver = false;
draw_set_font(fnt_HUD);
```

3. Add a **DrawGUI** event (under **Draw**) and place a code block in the **Actions** box.

4. Enter this code:

```
draw_text(32, 32, string("Health: ") + string(global.
playerHealth));
draw_text(32, 64, string("Lives: ") + string(global.playerLives));
scoreString = string(global.playerScore);
stringLength = 6 - string_length(scoreString);
stringTemp = "";
while(stringLength > 0)
{
    stringTemp += "0";
    stringLength -= 1;
}
scoreString = stringTemp + scoreString;
draw_text(room_width - 96, 32, scoreString);
```

5. In obj_gameControl, add a **Create** event.

6. Place the following code in a code block:

```
global.enemy = 0;
global.enemyMax = 10;
alarm[0] = 30;
instance_create(room_width/2, room_height/2, obj_base);
```

7. Add an event to **Alarm 0** using the following code:

```
spawn_point = choose(0, 1, 2, 3)
if (spawn_point = 0)
{
    instance_create(-64,random(room_height), obj_enemy);
}
if (spawn_point = 1)
{
    instance_create((room_width+64), random(room_height), obj_
enemy);
}
if (spawn_point = 2)
{
    instance_create(random(room_width), -64, obj_enemy);
}
if (spawn_point = 3)
{
    instance_create(random(room_width), (room_height+64), obj_
enemy);
}
alarm[0] = 45;
```

8. Add a **Step** event and drag a code block to the **Actions** box.

9. Enter the following code:

```
if global.playerHealth <= 0
{
    global.playerLives -= 1;
    global.playerHealth = 100;
}
if global.playerLives <= 0
{
    global.gameOver = true;
}
if global.gameOver
{
    game_restart();
}
```

10. In obj_enemy, add a **Create** event to the following code:

```
move_towards_point(obj_base.x, obj_base.y, 5);
```

11. Add a **Step** event and place a code block in the **Actions** box.

12. Enter the following code:

```
if mouse_check_button_pressed(mb_left)
{
    if instance_position(mouse_x, mouse_y, obj_enemy)
    {
        global.playerScore += 10;
        instance_destroy();
    }
}
```

13. Add a **Collision** event to obj_base and use the following code:

```
global.playerHealth -= 25;
instance_destroy();
```

Now, simply place one instance each of obj_display and obj_gameControl anywhere in the room and you're set. There is no need to place an instance of obj_base, as this will be handled by the code in order to place it in the exact center of the room. If you wish to place the base elsewhere in the room or in multiple places, simply adjust the code or erase it and place the objects manually. When you test the game, simply click on the enemies before they reach your base and collect points. As enemies collide with your base, it will lose health. When it runs out of health, you'll lose a life.

How it works

This simple game demonstrates the basics of GameMaker's GUI layer and the **DrawGUI** event. **DrawGUI** renders to the application surface outside any draw events. Essentially, if you use **Draw** to render sprites or textures within the game, regardless of the depth, **DrawGUI** will render items on top of them. Not only that, it bases positions on the (0, 0) coordinates of the view, as opposed to the room. This makes it ideal for your HUD as it will follow the view instead staying put within the room. Even though **DrawGUI** events will supersede standard **Draw** events, you can still use layer items *within* **DrawGUI**, using the depth value as you would, normally.

In the **Create** event of `obj_display`, we used `draw_set_font` to change the font used when displaying any string we code. This prevents you from relying on GameMaker's default font and font settings and allows you to use a custom font, if you choose to create one. You'll notice that, when we set the font, it is used across any strings displayed on the screen. Do you want to use multiple fonts? You'll need to use multiple control objects and set a different font for each of them. If your game design calls for multiple fonts or styles, make sure to use descriptive naming conventions to avoid confusion.

In order to display health, life, and score values on the screen, we first need to convert them into strings. GameMaker must be told exactly what you wish to display, but it can display the value of any variable as a string alphanumerically. Since we want to display titles (that is, health, lives, and scores) as well as their values, we have to tell GameMaker to do so using the **+** sign. This allows us to display multiple titles or values without having to hardcode the positions of each after a lot of thought and confusion. You may also have noticed the use of the classic arcade scoring system with a finite number of potential digits. This was done on purpose for aesthetic reasons. By assigning the score value, the length (in digits) of that value and strings of the number 0, we were able to replace the zeros in these spaces with the actual score. It's a small price to pay for the layout you want. When your base runs out of lives, the game restarts, as we've seen in recipes from previous chapters. This isn't ideal from a game design perspective, but we'll get into remedies for this at a later point in this chapter.

These are some of the basics you can accomplish in terms of your user interface, but these simple functions coupled with custom graphics and your own creativity can make a great user experience.

Making your HUD scalable

Have you ever played a game that didn't quite fit your screen? It's frustrating, isn't it? In a perfect world, your game would work perfectly on any device. Since that's not the case, however, you'll need to make some adjustments if you want to create a game that will fit at least *most* devices. Let's see what it takes to scale your game to fit screens of different sizes and ratios.

Getting ready

For this recipe, we'll use the game that we created previously. Open the project file and follow the given steps, but make sure **Allow the player to resize the game window** is activated and **Keep aspect ratio** is selected under **Global Game Settings**.

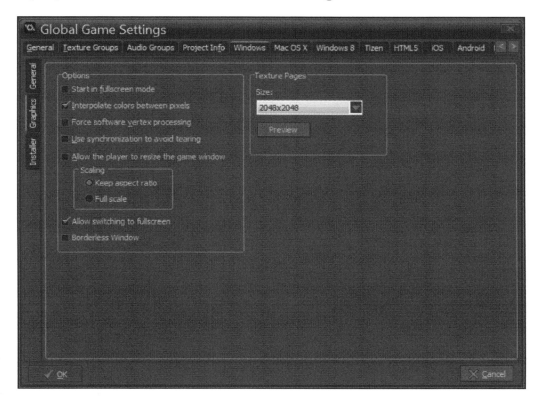

How to do it

1. Open `obj_display`.
2. Under the **DrawGUI** event, open the code block.
3. Enter the following code above the existing code:
   ```
   display_w = 1024;
   display_h = 768;
   ratio = display_get_width()/display_get_height();
   if ratio > 1
   {
   ```

```
        adjust_w = display_h * ratio;
        adjust_h = display_h;
        display_set_gui_size(display_h * ratio, display_h);
    }
    else
    {
        adjust_w = display_w;
        adjust_h = display_w/ratio;
        display_set_gui_size(display_w, display_w/ratio);
    }
```

4. Replace the last line of code with this code:

```
    draw_text(adjust_w - 96, 32, scoreString);
```

Once this is done, test the game and try resizing the player window.

How it works

When resizing the test window, you will notice a couple of things: Firstly, you will notice that the game's aspect ratio remains the same even when you change the size and shape of the player window. By selecting **Keep aspect ratio** in **Global Game Settings**, you're telling GameMaker to do exactly that. Regardless of the device you're using or the aspect ratio of the screen on which you're displaying your game, GameMaker will keep the game's aspect ratio intact. Conversely, if you select **Full scale**, GameMaker will squash and stretch the image to fit the display.

Secondly, you will notice that, as you resize the window and game itself, the GUI remains in its place in conjunction with the play area. To achieve this, we must find the dimensions of the display being used and use this information to resize the play area to fit the screen while maintaining the game's aspect ratio. The aspect ratio is calculated by taking the width of the window or displaying and dividing it by its height. This value is then used to find the adjusted width (for landscape mode) or height (for portrait mode). To find the new width, we need to multiply the original height by the aspect ratio; in order to find the new height, we need to divide the original width by the aspect ratio. These new values are used to set the GUI dimensions using `display_set_gui_size()`, as mentioned earlier. In order to make GameMaker alter the proper dimension, we must check the value of the ratio that we calculated. If the ratio is greater than 1, then the display's width is greater than its height and the display is therefore in landscape mode.

We can then use the original height and find the adjusted width by multiplying the original height by the value of the ratio, thus ensuring that the GUI will retain the original aspect ratio but with new dimensions. If the ratio is one or less, the width is less than the height, which means that the display is in portrait mode. Here, we keep the width and find the adjusted height by dividing the original width by the calculated value of the ratio, again keeping the aspect ratio intact while finding the new height.

Once we've found the adjusted width and height, we can then use them to draw our GUI. In our code, we used the adjusted width to place the score counter on the right-hand side of the screen, relative to the width of the display. Whenever the dimensions of the display area are altered, their positions are recalculated and the score is moved proportionately.

Using the GUI layer in full screen mode with views

When resizing the display, in order to keep the aspect ratio of the game screen (or application surface) intact, GameMaker will employ a letterbox to fill the rest of the screen. These black bars may be appropriate for your particular game, but in general they are not ideal; the black bars represent potentially wasted space. The letterbox is likely to be present when keeping the game's aspect ratio, unless the dimensions of the screen happen to match that of the room you created. For this reason, it is a good idea to employ views and allow GameMaker to change the size of these views depending on the display being used. Let's take a look at incorporating views for use in full screen mode in GameMaker.

Getting ready

Once again, we'll use the same game project we've been working with in this chapter. However, in order to ensure that every line of code ends up where it belongs, it will be easier to follow along from start to finish. Before we begin, it's important to know that, when adapting the view to fit a display (such as various mobile devices and tablets), unless the screen is exactly the same size as the room being displayed, there is a likelihood that the viewable area will either expand or contract. In order to accommodate this, it's good practice to use views that are slightly smaller than the rooms themselves.

To accomplish this, you need to allow the use of views, shrink the view to a smaller size (preferably with the same aspect ratio), and center it within the room.

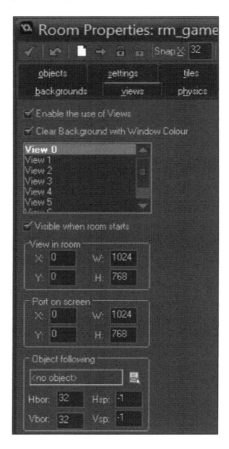

How to do it

1. In rm_game, under the **Settings** tab, click on the **Creation** code button.

2. Enter the following code:

```
display_w = 1024;
display_h = 768;
display_wMax = display_get_width();
display_hMax = display_get_height();
ratio = display_get_width()/display_get_height();
if (display_wMax < display_hMax)
{
```

```
        view_w = min(display_w, display_wMax);
        view_h = view_w/ratio;
    }
    else
    {
        view_h = min(display_h, display_hMax);
        view_w = view_h*ratio;
    }
    view_wview[0] = floor(view_w);
    view_hview[0] = floor(view_h);
    view_wport[0] = display_wMax;
    view_hport[0] = display_hMax;
    surface_resize(application_surface, view_wview[0], view_hview[0]);
```

3. In obj_display, add a **Create** event and drag a code block to the **Actions** box.

4. Enter the following code:

```
global.playerHealth = 100;
global.playerLives = 3;
global.playerScore = 0;
global.gameOver = false;
draw_set_font(fnt_HUD);
```

5. Add a **DrawGUI** event and enter the following code in a code block:

```
draw_text(32, 32, string("Health: ") + string(global.
playerHealth));
draw_text(32, 64, string("Lives: ") + string(global.playerLives));
scoreString = string(global.playerScore);
stringLength = 6 - string_length(scoreString);
stringTemp = "";
while(stringLength > 0)
{
    stringTemp += "0";
    stringLength -= 1;
}
scoreString = stringTemp + scoreString;
draw_text(display_get_gui_width() - 128, 32, scoreString);
```

6. In obj_gameControl, add a **Create** event to the following code and place a code block in the **Actions** box:

```
global.enemy = 0;
global.enemyMax = 10;
alarm[0] = 30;
instance_create(room_width/2, room_height/2, obj_base);
```

7. Add an event to **Alarm[0]** and drag a code block to the **Actions** box.

8. Enter this code:

```
spawn_point = choose(0, 1, 2, 3)
if (spawn_point = 0)
{
    instance_create(-64,random(room_height), obj_enemy);
}
if (spawn_point = 1)
{
    instance_create((room_width+64), random(room_height), obj_
enemy);
}
if (spawn_point = 2)
{
    instance_create(random(room_width), -64, obj_enemy);
}
if (spawn_point = 3)
{
    instance_create(random(room_width), (room_height+64), obj_
enemy);
}
alarm[0] = 45;
```

9. Add a **Step** event to the following code:

```
if global.playerHealth <= 0
{
    global.playerLives -= 1;
    global.playerHealth = 100;
}
if global.playerLives <= 0 {
    global.gameOver = true;
}
if global.gameOver
{
    game_restart();
}
```

10. In `obj_enemy`, add a **Create** event and place a code block in the **Actions** box.

11. Enter the following code:

```
move_towards_point(obj_base.x, obj_base.y, 5);
```

12. Add a **Step** event.

13. Drag a code block to the **Actions** box and enter the following code:

```
if mouse_check_button_pressed(mb_left)
{
    if instance_position(mouse_x, mouse_y, obj_enemy)
    {
        global.playerScore += 10;
        instance_destroy();
    }
}
```

14. Add a **Collision** event to `obj_base`.

15. Place a code block in the **Actions** box and enter the following code:

```
global.playerHealth -= 25;
instance_destroy();
```

You can now test the game and play it by clicking on the enemies before they reach the base, but make sure to do this either on a device or by entering full screen mode (*Alt + Enter*) when you are testing on a PC.

How it works

Much of the code in this recipe works as it did in previous recipes; the game has enemies approaching your base and you must click on them to destroy them before they reach it. The score and player information are still displayed on the GUI layer, though in a slightly different way, thanks to some changes made to the display code, which is now housed within the room creation code.

As mentioned earlier, this code is used to allow a full screen gameplay for a variety of devices with varying aspect ratios. We must first establish the base dimensions of the game. In this case, we have a play area that is 1024 px wide by 768 px high. This information is used in conjunction with the maximum width and height of the play area, which are the dimensions of the display itself. We gather this information using the `display_get_width/height` functions. The width of the display is then divided by its height in order to get its aspect ratio, which is used in several places to alter the dimensions of the view and play area. As mentioned earlier, GameMaker must first determine whether the device is in landscape or portrait mode; it will determine which dimension to alter based on this outcome. We use the `min()` function to determine the lowest of a given set of values in order to scale the view.

In the case of a portrait view, the view width becomes the minimum value between the base width (the one we established) and the maximum width (the actual width of the display). This value is then divided by the aspect ratio value to determine the view's height. Conversely, in the case of a landscape display, we can find the view height by calculating the minimum value between the base height and maximum height, and then using this value to find the new view width by multiplying the view height by the aspect ratio. Once the view width and height are found, we can convert them into actual view dimensions using the floor (the given number rounded down to the nearest integer) of the returned view width and height. The view port is the area of the display where the view will be projected or drawn. Once the view is fully established, the application surface (the area to which all visuals in the game are to be drawn) is resized to match.

There's more

By creating a room larger than the view, you can be certain that, when the application surface is resized, no area will be drawn beyond what you created in the room. For example, my laptop screen has a wider aspect ratio than 1024 x 768. In fact, it's closer to 1280 x 768. So, when I run this code and enter full screen mode, GameMaker resizes the application surface and draws an area *beyond* the size of the room I initially created, leaving a blank area that was technically part of the game. This is also the reason why, when releasing a mobile game, testing on multiple devices is very important. If your game doesn't display properly on a popular device, you probably need to alter the room size as well as the views.

Adding a title screen

Of all the games you've ever played in your life, how many of them have jumped immediately to gameplay? Your answer is likely less than a few, if any. Any game that I can remember playing, personally, has had at least a title screen, if not several splash screens indicating the studios and publishers involved in the game's creation. Now, I understand why. Jumping right into gameplay without context can throw you into the mix before you're ready, causing confusion. I mean that you likely know what game you're playing at the time, but a title screen can at least set the mood or give you a clue as to what's about to happen when you start the game. In addition to this, title screens often house, or at least lead to, the main menu in which you can customize your experience, but we'll dive into this in the next chapter. For now, let's take a look at how to create a title screen.

Getting ready

Again, we will continue to use the game project in this chapter. This recipe will be simple, but you'll need a few things before we begin. We're going to make a title screen and main menu. You'll need a background image and sprites for the game's title (which you can assign to `obj_title`) and menu selections such as settings, back, play, and quit. You'll also need objects (with this naming scheme: `obj_btn_buttonName`) for each of these items, as well as `obj_titleControl` and `obj_settings`. You'll also need two new rooms called `rm_title` and `rm_settings`, and the room creation code from the previous recipe should be the same across every room. Since GameMaker starts in the first room listed, it's important that `rm_title` is first listed in the asset explorer.

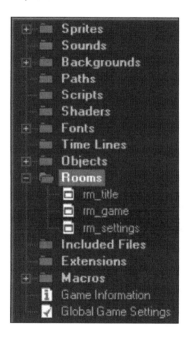

How to do it

1. Open `obj_titleControl` and add a **Create** event.

2. Place a code block in the **Actions** box and add the following code:

   ```
   instance_create(room_width/2, 280, obj_title);
   instance_create(room_width/2, 450, obj_btn_play);
   instance_create(room_width/2, 495, obj_btn_settings);
   instance_create(room_width/2, 540, obj_btn_quit);
   ```

3. In `obj_settings`, add a **Create** event and drag a code block to the **Actions** box.

4. Enter the following code:

```
instance_create(room_width/2, 400, obj_btn_back);
```

5. Open `obj_btn_settings` and add a **Left Mouse Button Pressed** event.

6. In a code block, enter the following code:

```
room_goto(rm_settings);
```

7. Open `obj_btn_back` and add a **Left Mouse Button Pressed** event.

8. Place a code block in the **Actions** box and add the following code:

```
room_goto(rm_title);
```

9. In `obj_btn_quit`, add a **Left Mouse Button Pressed** event and place a code block in the **Actions** box.

10. Enter the following code:

```
game_end();
```

11. In `obj_btn_play`, add a **Left Mouse Button Pressed** event.

12. Place a code block in the **Actions** box and add the following code:

```
room_goto(rm_game);
```

The following steps should be completed for each of the button objects:

1. Add a **Mouse Enter** event and drag a code block to the **Actions** box.

2. Enter the following code:

```
image_xscale += 1;
image_yscale += 1;
```

3. Add a **Mouse Leave** event with a code block.

4. Enter the following code:

```
image_xscale -= 1;
image_yscale -= 1;
```

Once all the steps are completed, test the program and play around with the buttons. The buttons should allow you to navigate to and from the **Settings** menu, play the game, or quit the program altogether.

How it works

GameMaker makes creating branching screens and a menu system quite simple. Thanks to the use of rooms and code embedded within objects, moving from one screen to another is a snap. As you can see, navigating from the title screen to the settings menu, or even right to the gameplay, is as simple as calling the `room_goto()` function in conjunction with the room to which you wish to jump. This function can be called in many ways, the most common way being a mouse click or button press. One thing you must keep in mind is that, when you move from one room to another, the room will begin fresh from the start, as if loaded for the first time. This happens even if you've been to that room previously. When you go from the title screen to the settings screen, the title screen you were on isn't saved; rather, it's destroyed in order to save memory. Then, when you go back to the title screen by clicking on the **Back** button, the title screen you see now is brand new and runs from the first line of code. This can be an issue if you wish to have gameplay that features moving from one room to another, but this problem can be circumvented by saving and recalling the game data, which we'll discuss in the next chapter.

Creating splash pages

When you start a video game, especially a modern game, you'll often be greeted by one or several images or animations telling you who made the game (or even who made certain engines that were used to make the game). These splash pages are important to the developers because they want you to remember them when choosing your next game; if you liked the game they made, why not choose another by the same developer/publisher? Think of it as the information you see on the screen at the beginning of a movie; this recognition is important for everyone involved in making the movie happen. Now, some splash screens are simple images, such as the studio's logo or even simple text (though images are certainly more effective, in my opinion). Others involve an animated version of the studio's logo or even audio. Have you ever played an EA Sports game? When the EA logo shows up, you get an intense voice telling you "EA Sports. It's in the game!" It's the same across all EA Sports games because they want this ingrained in your head so that you'll remember it the next time you're looking to make a purchase. Let's add some splash screens to the game so that you can put your name on it.

Getting ready

We'll continue with the game in this chapter, so make sure it's loaded in GameMaker. You'll need two splash screens: one with an image (perhaps your logo or just your name) and one with an animation. The image could be a sprite attached to an object, but for this recipe we'll simply make the object the background. For the animation, place it in a sprite and attach this sprite to an object called `obj_animLogo`. As for the splash screens themselves, they should each be rooms called `rm_splash_01` and `rm_splash_02`. Order them in the asset explorer *before* `rm_title` (from the previous recipe) and make sure `rm_splash_01` has the logo as its background. You'll also need control objects called `obj_splashControl_01` and `obj_splashControl_02`.

How to do it

1. Open `obj_animLogo`.
2. Add a **Create** event and drag a code block to the **Actions** box.
3. Enter the following code:

    ```
    image_speed = 0.8;
    ```

4. Click on **Add Event**, then **Other**, and select **Animation End**.
5. In a code block, add the following code:

    ```
    room_goto(rm_title);
    ```

6. Close `obj_animLogo` and open `obj_splashControl_01`.
7. Add a **Create** event and drag a code block to the **Actions** box.
8. Enter the following code:

    ```
    alarm[0] = 180;
    ```

9. Add an event to **Alarm 0**.
10. Place a code block in the **Actions** box using the following code:

    ```
    room_goto(rm_splash_02);
    ```

11. Add a **Step** event and place a code block in the **Actions** box.
12. Enter the following code:

    ```
    if keyboard_check_pressed(vk_space)
    {
        room_goto(rm_splash_02);
    }
    ```

13. In `obj_splashControl_02`, add a **Create** event to the following code:

```
instance_create(room_width/2, room_height/2, obj_animLogo);
alarm[0] = 180;
```

14. Add an event to **Alarm 0** and place a code block in the **Actions** box.

15. Enter the following code:

```
room_goto(rm_title);
```

16. Add a **Step** event to the following code:

```
if keyboard_check_pressed(vk_space)
{
    room_goto(rm_title);
}
```

Once these steps are complete, make sure each splash page has its respective control object and you're set.

How it works

For this recipe, we used two splash pages but this number is arbitrary. You can add as many as you like with whatever you want on each one. Do you remember arcade machines? Many of them had splash pages with legal information or even the infamous "Winners don't use drugs." page. The point of this recipe was to demonstrate a few ways to transition from one room to another. Firstly, we set a timer via an Alarm event. When the timer hits the predetermined value, GameMaker follows the instructions which, in this case, are to move on to the next room. Secondly, we added a **Step** event whose sole instruction is to check whether the spacebar has been pressed or not. In the event that it *has* been pressed, GameMaker's instructions are to move on the next room. Essentially, we just allow the player to skip through the splash page (instead of waiting) in order to get to the game. Thirdly, and this applies only to animated logos, we used the **Animation End** event in conjunction with the animated logo object. Again, the player can skip through this using the spacebar, but instead of waiting for a timer, GameMaker simply waits for the animation to end. Once the last frame is drawn, GameMaker follows the instructions to move on to the next room which, in this case, is the game's title page. Now, something to keep in mind here is that, while you can make the animation as short or as long as you want, it will only be visible as long as it is playing. In order to ensure that the player sees your logo (assuming he/she doesn't skip it), you can either make the animation long enough for the player to take in the information, or you can combine the Animation End event with an Alarm event. Instead of calling the `room_goto()` function, you can have GameMaker set an alarm, at the end of which GameMaker will finally call `room_goto()`. This way is much easier as it does not involve a longer animation, which is more work for the artist and takes up more memory.

There's more

The methods outlined in this recipe don't apply only to splash and title pages; you can use these methods in the game as well. Imagine a puzzle game where, once the final event of a puzzle is solved, GameMaker moves on to another room. What if, once a certain item is collected or a specific score is reached, the player is whisked off to a bonus round? Moving from one room to another allows you to set up more elaborate gameplay elements that, if properly utilized, can add a lot of depth to a game. Now, in order to properly incorporate these methods into an actual gameplay and allow the player to move from one room to another and back again, you'll need to know how to save and recall a game's data and/or a player's stats, but this will be covered in the next chapter. In the meantime, think of this when designing your next game or gameplay mechanic.

Adding a game over screen

How do you know when you've lost the game you're playing? Well, if you're playing the game we've been creating in this chapter, you will know this because it resets itself. Not very appealing from a player's standpoint, right? Most games will show you a game over screen that will, at the very least, tell you that your gameplay session has finished. Let's take a look at creating a game over screen and what information we can convey to the player.

Getting ready

We're going to finish our game with a game over screen, so make sure that the project file is open. You'll need a few things before we begin, so let's take a look at the list. First, you'll need a new room called `rm_gameOver`. You'll also need a controller object called `obj_gameOverCtrl` as well as objects called `obj_btn_exit` and `obj_btn_restart`. We'll be reusing `obj_btn_quit`, but this will be available since we're using the same game project.

How to do it

1. In `rm_gameOver`, open the creation code and enter the following code:

```
ddisplay_w = 1024;
display_h = 768;
display_wMax = display_get_width();
display_hMax = display_get_height();
ratio = display_get_width()/display_get_height();
if (display_wMax < display_hMax)
{
```

```
        view_w = min(display_w, display_wMax);
        view_h = view_w/ratio;
    }
    else
    {
        view_h = min(display_h, display_hMax);
        view_w = view_h*ratio;
    }
    view_wview[0] = floor(view_w);
    view_hview[0] = floor(view_h);
    view_wport[0] = display_wMax;
    view_hport[0] = display_hMax;
    surface_resize(application_surface, view_wview[0], view_hview[0]);
    instance_create(view_w/2, (view_h/2)-64, obj_btn_restart);
    instance_create(view_w/2, view_h/2, obj_btn_exit);
```

2. instance_create(view_w/2, (view_h/2)+64, obj_btn_quit); In `obj_gameOverCtrl`, add a **DrawGUI** event.

3. Drag a code block to the **Actions** box and enter the following code:

```
draw_text((display_get_gui_width()/2)-64, (display_get_gui_
height()/2)-200, string("Score: ") + string(global.playerScore));
```

4. In `obj_btn_restart`, add a **Left Mouse Button Pressed** event.

5. Place a code block in the **Actions** box using the following code:

```
room_goto(rm_game);
```

6. In `obj_btn_exit`, add a **Left Mouse Button Pressed** event and drag a code block to the **Actions** box.

7. Enter the following code:

```
room_goto(rm_title);
```

The following steps should be completed for each of the new button objects:

1. Add a **Mouse Enter** event and drag a code block to the **Actions** box.

2. Enter the following code:

```
image_xscale += 1;
image_yscale += 1;
```

3. Add a **Mouse Leave** event.

4. Place a code block in the **Actions** box and enter the following code:

```
image_xscale -= 1;
image_yscale -= 1;
```

5. Finally, in the **Step** event of `obj_gameControl`, locate this code:

```
if global.gameOver
{
    game_restart();
}
```

6. Replace the preceding code with this code:

```
if global.gameOver
{
    room_goto(rm_gameOver);
}
```

Once these steps are completed, make sure that an instance of `obj_gameOverCtrl` is placed in `rm_gameOver` and you're all set. When you play the game, if you allow yourself to lose, you'll see your score for the game as well as a few options. Play for a few times to try each of the buttons.

How it works

The final recipe in this chapter combines elements of all of the previous recipes involved in making our game. The code we entered in the creation code for `rm_gameOver` is largely the same as in the other rooms, but here, we've added a few extras. By piggybacking on this code with the `instance_create` code for the button objects, we can utilize the variables created here. Using the `view_w` and `view_h` variables, we can ensure that the objects are created in relation to what will be viewed on the screen and therefore always in the same viewing space.

The real purpose of the game over room is to tie the game together and make it feel like an actual game. The Draw GUI event called in the control object displays the score based on the global `playerScore` variable from the game room. This shows the player how well he/she did and can encourage him/her to try again and improve the score. The buttons displayed can be used to quit the game by calling `game_end`, jumping to the title, or even playing again by reloading the game room with `room_goto(rm_game)`. All of the game elements from this chapter collaborate to create a cohesive game experience. It may not be an AAA blockbuster but it's a game that works. The next few chapters will be dedicated to taking a simple game and adding polish to it.

7
Saving the Day – Saving Game Data

In this chapter, we'll cover the following topics:

- ▶ Creating game settings
- ▶ Making a pause screen
- ▶ Saving player selection and score
- ▶ Encrypting and decrypting save data

Introduction

Even though they work mostly in the background, save systems play a huge role in games. Be it saving your game progress, tracking your object positions, or even keeping your high score, saving data is crucial to game development. It may not be exciting or glamorous but it's the truth. Would you keep playing a game in which you collect weapons, experience points, and artifacts, only to have them disappear when you go to the next stage? No, you'd likely shut it off and go back to playing something else. Keeping track of information can allow your players to save their progress and come back to it some other time, or even compete with other players for arcade supremacy (this means having the highest score). Let's see what it takes to build these systems and implement them in your game.

Background data

Okay, let's start with the boring, behind-the-scenes stuff. Here, we'll take a look at how to save and recall bits of information as they pertain to game elements and settings:

- ▸ Creating game settings
- ▸ Making a pause screen

Save systems

Due to the difficulty or amount of content, sometimes you just can't finish a game in one sitting. For this reason, we have save systems. We'll take a look at how to save and recall player stats:

- ▸ Saving player selection and score
- ▸ Encrypting and decrypting save data

Creating game settings

I've noticed with modern games that I don't always like the default settings in terms of sound, visuals, controls, or even difficulty. I always go through the options menu to adjust everything and I know I'm not alone. It is because of this desire to customize your play experience that game developers add these options to the games they create. Now, this can be something as simple as controlling the music volume or as complicated as setting custom control macros, but I find how I play to be important. Let's take a look at how we can create a simple settings menu with audio options.

Getting ready

For this recipe, you can continue with the game from the previous chapter, or you can start with a new one. Either way, you'll need three rooms: `rm_splash`, `rm_title`, and `rm_settings`, in this particular order. As before, set `rm_splash` to move on to `rm_title` after a few seconds or once you hit the Spacebar. Your title screen should have a **Settings** button (`obj_btn_settings`) that leads the player to `rm_settings`. In the settings screen, you should already have a **Back** button (`obj_btn_back`) that leads back to `rm_title`, but we can add more to this screen for reasons that should be obvious.

With this out of the way, you can begin gathering some necessities. You'll need two sound files: one music (`snd_msc_background`) and one sound effect (`snd_sfx_chime`). In reality, you can rename these sounds to whatever you think is relevant, but you'll need to remember this when referencing them in your code. You'll need a controller object called `obj_titleControl`, which does not require a sprite. You'll need volume control buttons: `obj_btn_mscVolUp`, `obj_btn_mscVolDown`, `obj_btn_sfxVolUp`, and `obj_btn_sfxVolDown`. The naming scheme may seem a little long-winded, but it's important to label everything as descriptively as possible to avoid confusion when debugging. You'll also need a **Save** button with an appropriate sprite (`obj_btn_save`).

To represent your volume levels, you'll need sound effects and music volume bars (`obj_mscVol` and `obj_sfxVol`). The sprites for each of these will be very similar with the label being the only difference. Each should have 11 frames (0-10) with frame `0` being nothing more than the label. Frames 1-10 will represent the volume levels visually: frame 1 will have one bar and frame 10 will have 10 bars. It is very important for the frame with zero bars to be represented by frame 0 of the sprite.

Finally, you'll need to make a change to your PC's filesystem; you need to disable hiding the file extension. In most versions of Windows, this can be accomplished by opening **folder options** (this can be searched for from the **Start** menu), clicking on the **View** tab, and making sure **Hide extensions for known file types** is *not* checked.

With all of this prep work done, we can begin coding our settings screen.

How to do it

1. Open GameMaker's local storage folder. By default, this is located at `C:/Users/<Username>/AppData/Local/<GameMaker project name>`.

2. In this folder, create a Notepad file, name it `Settings.ini`, and make sure that the file type has changed to `Configuration settings`.

3. Open `Settings.ini` and add the following code:

   ```
   [Sound]
   sfxVol=5
   musicVol=5
   ```

4. In GameMaker, open `rm_splash`.

5. In the `Creation` code, add the following code:

   ```
   global.music_emit = audio_emitter_create();
   global.sfx_emit = audio_emitter_create();
   ```

6. Open `rm_title` and `rm_settings` and enter the following code in the `Creation` code for each room:

```
ini_open('Settings.ini');
global.musicVol = ini_read_real('Sound', 'musicVol', 3);
global.sfxVol = ini_read_real('Sound', 'sfxVol', 3);
ini_close();
global.music_gain = global.musicVol*0.1;
global.sfx_gain = global.sfxVol*0.1;
audio_emitter_gain(global.music_emit, global.music_gain)
audio_emitter_gain(global.sfx_emit, global.music_gain);
```

7. In `obj_titleControl`, add the following code to the **Create** event:

```
if !audio_is_playing(snd_msc_background)
{
    audio_play_sound_on(global.music_emit, snd_msc_background,
true, 1);
}
```

8. Open `obj_mscVol` and add a **Create** event using the following code:

```
ini_open("Settings.ini");
image_index = ini_read_real("Sound", "musicVol",1);
ini_close();
```

9. Add a **Step** event using the following code in a code block:

```
image_index = global.musicVol;
```

10. Repeat the two previous steps and replace `musicVol` with `sfxVol`.

11. In `obj_btn_mscVolUp`, add a **Left Mouse Button Pressed** event using the following code:

```
if global.musicVol < 10
{
    global.musicVol += 1;
    global.music_gain = global.musicVol*0.1;
    audio_emitter_gain(global.music_emit, global.music_gain);
}
```

12. In `obj_btn_mscVolDown`, add a **Left Mouse Button Pressed** event using this code:

```
if global.musicVol > 0
{
    global.musicVol -= 1;
    global.music_gain = global.musicVol*0.1;
    audio_emitter_gain(global.music_emit, global.music_gain);
}
```

13. Repeat the last two steps with `obj_btn_sfxVolUp` and `obj_btn_sfxVolDown`, replace each instance of the word `music` with `sfx`, and add the following code on the line below the emitter gain function:

```
audio_play_sound_on(global.sfx_emit, snd_sfx_chime, false, 1);
```

14. In `obj_btn_save`, add a **Left Mouse Button Pressed** event using the following code:

```
ini_open('Settings.ini');
ini_write_real('Sound', 'musicVol', global.musicVol);
ini_write_real('Sound', 'sfxVol', global.sfxVol);
ini_close();
```

Once these steps are complete, place the save button and volume buttons and bars in `rm_settings`, and make sure an instance of `obj_titleControl` is in `rm_title`. You can now test your settings menu and play around with the sound and music volumes. Try exiting the title screen with and without saving.

How it works

This code may seem busy but we're going to focus on two main ideas: reading from and writing to the `.ini` files. Using variables, GameMaker stores information while the game is running. Once you exit, however, this information is lost. You can use the `.ini` files to store and load the information you want GameMaker to use even if you stop and restart the application. This is great to store values for settings such as we did here with volume levels.

When an `.ini` file is called in GameMaker, if the file does not yet exist, it will be created and populated with the information as it is set in the function. In this recipe, we created our own `.ini` settings file in GameMaker's local data folder. This allows you to have greater control over how the data within is organized, making it a best practice in my opinion. When we created our `.ini` file, we entered some information we wished to use in our project. We first entered the section, `[Sound]`. Sections allow you to organize like information. Under the sound section, we entered two keys: `musicVol` and `sfxVol`. Keys are where we store the actual values we wish to load and save.

Once our `Settings.ini` file is in place, GameMaker can reference it in order to pull values for our variables. In our case, we used these values to store and recall volume levels, which we then used to set the initial gain (volume) for our audio emitters. To read these values, GameMaker must first access the `.ini` file. To do this, we use `ini_open` (filename). This will open the file, giving GameMaker access to the goodies inside. By this, of course, I mean the data. The delicious data. Ahem, where was I? Right, the `.ini` files. Anyway, with the file open, we used `variable = ini_read_real("section", "key", default value)` to retrieve the specified numerical value and pass it to the variable we referenced. Notice that the section and key are in quotation marks.

This is because you're telling GameMaker to search for an exact string so that it can locate the value you want. While GameMaker reads the section and key as a string, with `ini_read_ real`, it cannot pass a string but only a variable. This is perfect for our uses here, as we just want to assign a new value to our volume variables. Lastly, we need to enter a default value. How will GameMaker create the `.ini` file we want if none exists in the appropriate directory? Well, we need to provide a default value that GameMaker can assign the key you're requesting for if it doesn't yet exist. This eliminates errors stemming from nonexistent data.

Now, with our new settings menu, we can raise and lower the volume for the game's music and sound effects. If you were to alter these settings and simply go back to the title screen, what would happen? The volume levels you changed would revert to their values before you changed them. This was a deliberate decision for a couple of reasons. Firstly, we don't want any unwanted changes to be saved. Secondly, while the global variables will remember the volume levels that we set for the remainder of play, what we really want is to have the game remember them the next time we want to play, so that we don't have to mess around with the settings again. For this, we must write the new values to the `.ini` file to be recalled the next time we play it. How do we do that? We use `ini_write_real`. Makes sense, right? Good. Now, since pressing the volume buttons alters the value of our sound effects and music volume variables, we need to write these same variables to the `.ini` file in order to preserve them. Using `ini_write_real("section", "key", variable)`, we can replace the former value of the key with the new value of the appropriate variable, thus saving it for the next time the `.ini` file is loaded.

Lastly, when we're done reading and/or writing to and from the `.ini` file, we need to close the file before we move on. If the file is left open, it will stay open, potentially causing memory leaks and leading to a slowdown or a program crash. For this, we simply use `ini_close()`. One thing to remember is that this is all done in the same step. You're not going to notice the file being opened and closed, but leaving a file open will take its toll.

There's more

In this recipe, you may have noticed that we used emitters for the sound, even though we had only two sounds. Here are a couple of things in this topic: firstly, we created both the emitters in the `Creation` code of `rm_splash`. The reason I did this is to ensure that these emitters were created and passed on to global variables *before* the title page was loaded, as they would be used right away. I find this to be a best practice when something needs to be preloaded to ensure that it is ready when it is needed. The splash screen isn't doing much else, right? Why not put it to work?

Secondly, the reason we used emitters is because we had two different types of sounds: music and sound effects. If you want one volume control for everything, you can forego the emitters altogether and simply use `audio_master_gain(gain)`. This will set the gain for all sounds of any kind, globally, within your game. GameMaker *does* have the ability to set audio groups (found in the **Global Game Settings** and utilized in the sound properties editor), but at the time of writing this book, it is still a buggy system. In my experience, audio groups can allow you to load and unload groups of sounds, as well as set their properties (such as gain), but the audio files don't always follow the rules you set. For this reason, I chose to use emitters, as you can set their properties individually and assign sound files to them on-the-fly. Putting together a sound profile for your game gives it great versatility.

Making a pause screen

What's worse than having someone interrupt you while you're playing a game you can't pause? That's right, nothing. That's why I'm sure that you'd like to add a game pause feature to the game you're working on. Let's take a look at a simple way to create a great looking pause screen.

Getting ready

We're just going to take a look at the functionality of this feature, so you won't need much for this recipe. Before I began, I created one room and placed several ball objects in it that move in random directions and bounce off the walls. Why did I do this? It's because this feature is best demonstrated with moving objects, not unlike a real game. Oh, and I made them speed up whenever they bump into a wall or each other. This part isn't important; I just thought it was more fun.

What you'll really need in order to make this work is two objects: `obj_control` and `obj_pause`. Neither of these objects requires a sprite, as they are both control objects, working in the background.

How to do it

1. Open `obj_control` and add a **Step** event.
2. Place a code block in the **Actions** box and enter the following code:

```
if keyboard_check_pressed(vk_escape)
{
    instance_create(x, y, obj_pause);
}
```

3. In `obj_pause`, add a **Create** event to a code block containing the following code:

```
screen_save("pauseBackground.png");
instance_deactivate_all(true);
pauseBackground = sprite_add("pauseBackground.png", 1, false,
false, 0, 0);
```

4. Add a **Draw** event and drag a code block to the **Actions** box.

5. Enter the following code:

```
draw_sprite(pauseBackground, 1, 0, 0);
draw_set_color(c_black);
draw_set_alpha(0.6);
draw_rectangle(0, 0, room_width, room_height, 0);
draw_set_alpha(1);
draw_set_color(c_white);
draw_text(room_width/2, room_height/2, "Paused");
draw_set_color(c_black);
```

6. Add a **Step** event to the following code in a code block:

```
if keyboard_check_pressed(vk_escape)
{
    instance_activate_all();
    instance_destroy();
}
```

7. Add a **Destroy** event to the following code:

```
if file_exists("pauseBackground.png")
{
    file_delete("pauseBackground.png");
}
```

Once these steps are completed, make sure an instance of `obj_control` (but not `obj_pause`) is placed in the room and you're all set to test. You can pause and resume the game using the *Escape* key.

How it works

This is one of several ways to create a pause screen, but it's the one I find the most useful. The `instance_deactive_all(true)` and `instance_activate_all()` functions are really all that you need to pause and resume your game but they leave a lot to be desired. On its own, `instance_deactivate_all(true)` simply shuts everything off right where it is; you're left with nothing but the background. Using `instance_activate_all()`,everything starts going again, right from where you left off.

Handy, yes, but terribly boring. In order to make the pause screen more appealing, what we've done is used `screen_save` (filename) to take a screenshot of the game before everything was deactivated (while it was still visible) and saved it to the filesystem as a `.png`. This image was then loaded into a sprite and displayed onscreen using the **Draw** event. This is a simple way of displaying everything that was onscreen a moment ago as though it were *still* onscreen in a frozen state. To take things a little further, we then faded a black rectangle, which is the size of the screen, by changing the alpha value and printed **Paused** on top of it, all in the same **Draw** event. All of this gives the illusion that everything you see is frozen in place and then faded into the background. A little more polish and you've got yourself a professional looking pause screen!

One important piece of this puzzle, however, is that, when we resume the game after pausing, not only are we destroying `obj_pause` and the **Draw** event, but we're also checking for the `.png` file that we created using `screen_save()` and deleting it using `file_delete` (filename). This serves several purposes; most importantly, we're freeing up disc space and preventing file errors and future screenshots from being renamed improperly.

There's more

While this method of pausing your game is quite functional, there's actually a lot more you can do with it. By adding a pause menu, you can give your player access to other functions, such as settings and options or even a quit button to take you out of the game. All you need to do is have the menu populate in the **Create** event of `obj_pause` in the same way that you would create them on the game's title screen.

Saving player selection and score

I personally enjoy games with a lot of choice. I like having options that expand the game's scope and add replay value, but I also enjoy being able to play a game the way *I* want to play it. I'm certainly not the only person who feels this way, and for this reason, many game developers add appropriate options. Now, once I've made my selection and get into the game, what I *don't* want is to have to make those selections again; I want to save my choice and pick up right from where I left off. Let's take a look at how to select a player character and then save this selection, along with the player's score.

Getting ready

To complete this recipe, you'll need several objects, sprites, and so on. You'll need two sprites (or skins, as they can be called in such scenarios) to represent the player's character options. I've chosen **Red** (spr_charRed) and **Blue** (spr_charBlue) as these are the classic choices in some of my favorite team-based games. Next you'll need your player character (obj_player) and a couple of controller objects (obj_controlGame and obj_init). You'll need a coin object (obj_coin) and several button objects (obj_btn_load, obj_btn_play, obj_btn_redSelect, and obj_btn_blueSelect), all with appropriate sprites. You'll need three rooms in this order: rm_init, rm_charSelect, and rm_game. Lastly, you'll need to create a Save.ini file with a section called **Player** and keys called **Selected**, **Score**, **Character**, and **Display**.

How to do it

1. Open obj_init and add a **Create** event.
2. Drag a code block to the **Actions** box and enter the following code:
   ```
   globalvar playerSelect;
   playerSelect = spr_charBlank;
   globalvar playerDisplay;
   playerDisplay = "Please select a character.";
   globalvar playerIsSelected;
   playerIsSelected = false;
   globalvar playerScore;
   playerScore = 0;
   alarm[0] = 60;
   ```

3. Add an event to Alarm[0] and enter the following code in a code block:
   ```
   room_goto(rm_charSelect);
   ```

4. In obj_btn_redSelect, add a **Left Mouse Button Pressed** event to a code block.
5. Enter the following code:
   ```
   playerSelect = spr_charRed;
   playerDisplay = "Red"
   playerIsSelected = true;
   ```

6. Complete the previous two steps with obj_btn_blueSelect, but replace the code with the following code:
   ```
   playerSelect = spr_charBlue;
   playerDisplay = "Blue";
   playerIsSelected = true;
   ```

7. In `obj_player`, add a **Create** event to the following code:

```
sprite_index = playerSelect;
```

8. Add a **Step** event and place the following code in a code block:

```
if keyboard_check(vk_left)
{
    x-=7;
}
if keyboard_check(vk_right)
{
    x+=7;
}
if keyboard_check(vk_up)
{
    y-=7;
}
if keyboard_check(vk_down)
{
    y+=7;
}
```

9. Add a **Collision** event to `obj_coin`.

10. Place a code block in the **Actions** box and enter the following code:

```
playerScore +=1;
with (other)
{
    instance_destroy();
}
instance_create(random(room_width), random(room_height), obj_
coin);
```

11. In `obj_btn_load`, add a **Left Mouse Button Pressed** event to the following code:

```
ini_open("Save.ini");
playerScore = ini_read_real("Player", "Score", 0);
playerSelect = ini_read_real("Player","Character", -1);
playerDisplay = ini_read_string("Player", "Display", "Please
select a character.");
playerIsSelected = ini_read_real("Player", "Selected", false);
ini_close();
```

12. In `obj_btn_play`, add a **Left Mouse Button Pressed** event to the following code in a code block:

```
if playerIsSelected = true
{
    room_goto(rm_game);
}
else
{
    //do nothing
}
```

13. In `obj_controlGame`, add a **Create** event and place a code block in the **Actions** box.

14. Enter the following code:

```
instance_create(random(room_width), random(room_height), obj_coin);
```

15. Add a **Step** event to the following code in a code block:

```
if keyboard_check_pressed(ord('S'))
{
    ini_open("Save.ini");
    ini_write_real("Player", "Score", playerScore);
    ini_write_real("Player", "Character", playerSelect);
    ini_write_real("Player", "Selected", playerIsSelected);
    ini_write_string("Player", "Display", playerDisplay);
    ini_close();
}
```

16. Add a **Draw** event to the following code:

```
draw_text(32, 64, string("Score: ") + string(playerScore));
draw_text(32, 32, string("Player: ") + string(playerDisplay));
```

Lastly, place `obj_init` in `rm_init`, `obj_controlGame` in `rm_game`, and arrange your button objects in `rm_title`. You are now ready to test your creation. Try using the character selection buttons, then play the game and collect coins to increase your score. You can save your character selection and score by pressing S and recall it the next time you run the program using the **Load** button.

How it works

This recipe is mainly used to demonstrate two elements of saving with `.ini` files: storing strings and how they differ from storing numbers and game elements. Here, we've written the code in order to save four different values: player score, player character selection, whether a character is selected or not, and which character name should be displayed. You'll notice that, for the first three save functions, we used `ini_write_real()`: for the fourth function, we used `ini_write_string()`. To understand why we did this, let's take a look at the information we're trying to save. Obviously, when we save the player's score, we're looking at numbers, plain and simple.

As with saving volume levels, when we create the audio settings, we take a numerical value from the game and store it as a real value in the `.ini` file. When saving whether a character has been selected or not, we're using a `true` or `false` statement. GameMaker views this as a binary statement. There can be only one of two outcomes. You can easily store this information as `0` (`false`) or `1` (`true`), so it is therefore stored as a real value.

Next, when the player selects a character, we ask GameMaker to store a value to indicate which sprite should be used (how the player will be skinned). Like the true or false statement we just dealt with, this information is saved using `ini_write_real`, despite the fact that it is not observably recorded as a numerical value. This is because, when you call a sprite, you're calling the sprite's index, not the sprite's name. Have you ever noticed that when you use code to assign a sprite to an object, you use the `sprite_index` variable? It's because, even though you've given it a name, GameMaker reads your sprite as a number. This is why the default value of `playerSelect` (if no previous value exists in the given file) is `-1`. This value, if recalled, is passed on to `obj_player` and referenced under `sprite_index`. If the value of `sprite_index` is read as `-1`, there is no sprite assigned to the object.

Lastly, we have `playerDisplay`, which is saved using `ini_write_string`. As the function's name implies, we'll store a value as a string (words) instead of a real value (numbers and so on). Now, there are some things to remember when we save a string. As with all uses of string functions, you need to use quotation marks. This tells GameMaker to read the value exactly as it is shown. GameMaker doesn't actually know the meaning of the words you've written; otherwise, it would try to read it as code. Instead, GameMaker takes whatever is in the quotation marks as a specific chunk and passes this chunk off to wherever it needs to go. In our case, we pass on the name of the character the player has chosen to the `draw_text()` function in order to display it on the screen. When saving and loading information to and from variables, you are likely to use `ini_write_real()` in most cases. The `ini_write_string()` method is most useful when we save names and descriptors. Specifically, I would use this to save a name entered by the player or to save the status of a character, item, and so on in the game. For example, if a player unlocks a new character, you can change the information in the `.ini` file from `locked` to `unlocked`. If an **non-player character** (**NPC**) in your game is killed, you can save the word **dead** under the **status** key. Just remember that, especially here, spelling counts!

There's more

You may have noticed that, in this recipe, we used an object called `obj_init`. This is an initialization object, like the one used in previous recipes. As mentioned earlier, we used this object to create variables that we needed to incorporate right away. What we did differently, this time, is use `globalvar` to create variables instead of calling `global.variableName`. This, effectively, creates a global variable that can be used by any object in the game, just like adding `global` in front of a variable name. The difference is that, once you've initialized a variable using `globalvar`, you don't need to keep adding global in front of the variable for the rest of the game; it is already recognized as a global variable. Also, when initializing a variable this way, you don't have to assign a value right away. You simply inform GameMaker of its existence and prepare it to be used at a later time. This is why, with some of the global variables used in this recipe, we assign a value to the new variable on the next line. In these specific cases, we simply need to assign a value right away. Otherwise, we could have left the variable blank at the time.

One important thing to keep in mind when using global variables is that, whichever method you choose for a particular variable, you need to be consistent. If you initialize using `globalvar` and then call the same variable using `global.variableName`, you will encounter some potentially game-crashing bugs. GameMaker will not view them as the same variable and will stop compiling the code.

Encrypting and decrypting save data

Everybody has secrets, right? Well, sometimes secrets can be helpful, especially when you want to prevent anyone playing your game from messing with save and setting files. If you're reading this, then you have a healthy interest in creating games and programming. If you're interested in programming, or even just figuring out how programs work, you have likely browse through a game or application's files and open one in Notepad. Was it all nonsensical, gibberish, and random characters? I bet it was. This is because the file was encrypted. Developers need to encrypt the code in a program's files to make it unreadable in order to prevent a user from altering the code in any way and thus changing how the program works. In terms of games, imagine if, instead of playing the game as intended, a player changed some save files manually in order to unlock every item and achievement you worked so hard to code. Where's the fun in that? Well, you're in luck because GameMaker can help you encrypt your code and prevent those cheaters from doing what they do best. Let's take a look at encryption and decryption in GameMaker.

Getting ready

Before we complete this recipe, I suggest that you complete the previous recipe if you haven't already. We'll use the same code with some alterations to see how the save function works.

How to do it

1. Open obj_controlGame.

2. In the **Step** event, replace the existing code with the following code:

```
if keyboard_check_pressed(ord('S'))
{
    ini_open("Save.ini");
    saveScore = base64_encode(string(playerScore));
    saveSelect = base64_encode(string(playerSelect));
    saveSelected = base64_encode(string(playerIsSelected));
    saveDisplay = base64_encode(string(playerDisplay));
    ini_write_string("Player", "Score", saveScore);
    ini_write_string("Player", "Character", saveSelect);
    ini_write_string("Player", "Selected", saveSelected);
    ini_write_string("Player", "Display", saveDisplay);
    ini_close();
}
```

3. Open obj_btn_load.

4. In the **Left Mouse Button Pressed** event, replace the code with the following code:

```
ini_open("Save.ini");
loadScore = ini_read_string("Player", "Score", "0");
loadSelect = ini_read_string("Player","Character", "spr_
charBlank");
loadDisplay = ini_read_string("Player", "Display", "Please select
a character.");
loadSelected = ini_read_string("Player", "Selected", "false");
playerScore = real(base64_decode(loadScore));
playerSelect = real(base64_decode(loadSelect));
playerDisplay = real(base64_decode(loadDisplay));
playerIsSelected = real(base64_decode(loadSelected));
ini_close();
```

Once these simple steps have been completed, you can test your game once again. Select a character, enter the game, collect some coins, and save. Now, open Save.ini and check out the new values. Can't read it? Good!

How it works

In order to encrypt your code, GameMaker uses the Base64 methods. Base64 is a name given to any of the several binary-to-text encoding schemes that are commonly used to transmit binary data as a string, where the binary data cannot be read. Simply put, GameMaker takes the game's data and changes each character to one of 64 characters, most often represented by uppercase and lowercase letters (A-Z, a-z), single digits (0-9), and a few other characters. While Base64 is by no means a safe way to encrypt sensitive data (there are many web-based Base64 encoders/decoders that can be accessed in seconds) it is a deterrent to the average player. Most people will not see the encoded saved files and say "I'm going to decode this and mess around with it." So, while I wouldn't use Base64 to hide my banking information, I would certainly use it to keep players from accessing level 8 before they've earned it.

In order to encrypt our data, we must initialize more variables as placeholders and call them when loading. Let's take a look at how we encrypt the player's score. First, we create the `saveScore` variable and declare it as `base64_encode(string(playerScore))`. This function will take the value of the `playerScore` variable, change it to a string, and encrypt this string using Base64 (which changes each character, even spaces). This new string is then stored as the value of `saveScore`. We can then write this value to our `.ini` file but, as it is now in a string format, we must do so using `ini_write_string(saveScore)`. At this point, you can open `Save.ini` and check your score, but you won't be able to read it because it's encrypted!

Now in order to load these values back into GameMaker, we have to perform the process in reverse. We declare a new variable (`loadScore`) as `ini_read_string("Player", "Score", "0")`. This takes the value of `Score` (which is now a string, not a number) and loads it into the new `loadScore` variable. We then take the value of this new variable (again, a string, not a number) and decode it using `real(base64_decode(loadScore)`. What does this `real` mean? It means that we tell GameMaker to take the decoded string and turn it back into a real number. This number is then passed on to the `playerScore` variable, which is then displayed for all to see.

You now have encryption and decryption in GameMaker. If you're still uncertain as to what Base64 really is, I highly recommend that you do a little bit of research on its history and check out some of the online encoders/decoders.

8
Light 'em up! – Enhancing Your Game with Lighting Techniques

In this recipe, we'll cover the following topics:

- ▶ Creating a room with a light switch
- ▶ Lighting objects with a spot light
- ▶ Changing day to night
- ▶ Creating a flashlight
- ▶ Making a flickering torch

Introduction

Game design trends, much like trends in fashion and music, are quite cyclical. There is currently a trend in game art, especially in indie circles, to give games a pixilated, retro feel but with modern game mechanics and effects. Many developers are trying to capture the look and feel of classic 8-bit and 16-bit games while simultaneously keeping the games modern using certain special effects. One of these effects is to give games lighting systems that can produce, in a way, realistic light effects, watered down as necessary to maintain the desired look.

This isn't *entirely* a new concept; some games from the 16-bit era had some basic lighting effects, though they were presented differently. Consider a couple of very popular games, such as the Super Nintendo Entertainment System: *Super Mario World* and *Legend of Zelda: A Link to the Past*. Both of these games used the same hardware and were released one year apart, almost to the day.

Super Mario World contains many levels that take place underground or indoors. This would be a perfect situation in which some basic lighting effects could add a lot of depth. Despite this, Mario and his enemies are lit (fairly brightly) consistently.

Conversely, in *The Legend of Zelda: A Link to the Past,* Link employs a lantern to light up dark areas. In this recipe, we'll take a look at how we can recreate this and several other lighting techniques that will add depth to your game and draw players into the game's world.

Before we begin, I have to mention that the effects laid out in this chapter are *not* examples of real game lighting. GameMaker does not come stocked with an advanced lighting engine. These recipes demonstrate ways to create effects that give the *illusion* of in-game objects being lit by an external source. To get true, real-time lighting in GameMaker requires the use of third-party extensions called shaders, which can be purchased from the GameMaker Marketplace.

Basic lighting

We all have to start somewhere. Luckily, starting here will set the pace and start you on your way to lighting your GameMaker projects. We'll begin with these simple effects:

- Creating a room with a light switch
- Lighting objects with a spot light

Light transitions

Have you ever been outside for an extended period of time or at least near a window? If you have (and I'm going to go ahead and guess that you have), then you will know that light changes as the day goes by. Dim lights and objects in the world around you take on new appearances as less light reaches them.

We'll take a look at how to recreate this effect in your game:

- Changing day to night

Light effects

What do you do when the power goes out at night? If you say "scream and then cower in the corner, sobbing quietly," then don't worry, I know how you feel. Like most people, you would probably opt to light a candle or grab a flashlight. Let's learn how to add these options in GameMaker:

> ▸ Creating a flashlight
>
> ▸ Making a flickering torch

Creating a room with a light switch

There are many things we take for granted in our day-to-day lives. One of those things is being able to light up a room at the flip of a switch; we don't really notice when it works as expected. It's not until we go to turn on a light and find that the bulb has burnt out, that we realize just how important this part of our life really is. The same can be said about lighting in games. If you can see everything in the game, you won't be worried about lights. If everything is dark, however, you'll be looking for a way to light up the play area so that you can navigate. Before we start creating lighting effects in GameMaker, let's take a look at lighting a game area, as simply as flipping a switch.

Getting ready

For this recipe, you'll need a room (rm_game), a character who can move using the arrow keys (obj_player), a box object (obj_box), and a controller object (obj_lightControl).

How to do it

1. In obj_lightControl, add a **Create** event.

2. Drag a code block to the **Actions** box and enter the following code:

   ```
   alpha = 0.95;
   darkSurface = surface_create(room_width, room_height);
   ```

3. Add a **Draw** event to another code block.

4. Enter the following code:

   ```
   surface_set_target(darkSurface);
   draw_clear(c_black);
   surface_reset_target();
   draw_surface_ext(darkSurface, 0, 0, 1, 1, 0, c_white, alpha);
   ```

5. Add a **Step** event.

6. Place a code block in the **Actions** box using this code:

```
if keyboard_check_pressed(vk_space) && alpha > 0
{
    alpha = 0;
}
else if keyboard_check_pressed(vk_space) && alpha = 0
{
    alpha = 0.95;
}
```

7. Set the depth of `obj_lightControl` to `-1` (or any other number that is lower than all the other objects in the room).

Once this is complete, add an instance each of `obj_lightControl` and `obj_player` to `rm_game` and place instances of `obj_box` in various places around the room. You can now test this recipe by moving your player around the obstacles and turning the lights on and off using the Spacebar key.

How it works

In this recipe, we've mocked up having a light turn on and off through the use of a surface. We don't actually see any light source, but we are given the sense that the room is being darkened or illuminated whenever we use the Spacebar key.

We created the `darkSurface` variable to represent `surface_create(w, h)` with the width and height set as the width and height of our room. This way, the surface will cover the entire room without existing beyond the playable area. This saves a great deal of memory when implementing surfaces.

In the **Draw** event, which does exactly what its name implies, we used `surface_set_target(index)` with `darkSurface`, which is set as the target. This tells GameMaker that we wish to draw to `darkSurface` rather than the screen itself.

We used `draw_clear(colour)` to clear the surface of everything but the given color, for which we chose black (called in GameMaker `c_black`). We have now set `darkSurface` as a black screen and set it on top of everything else on the screen.

Next, we have to revert the draw target back to the screen itself in order to prevent drawing to our new surface any further. We do this using `surface_reset_target()`, which reverts the draw target back to the screen as it is the default target.

We redraw our surface with the new settings by calling it using `draw_surface_ext(index, x, y, xscale, yscale, rot, color, alpha)`. Here, we set the *x* and *y* coordinates of the surface to `0`, which means that it will draw from the top-left corner of the screen. We also set the *x* scale and *y* scale to `1`, which orients the surface frontwards (setting them to `-1` would reverse it) and sets the rotation to `0`.

Finally, we set the blend color to white and set the `alpha` to the value of our `alpha` variable. With these last two values, we are blending the black color of the surface with white, thus changing the opacity in accordance with the `alpha` value.

Now, since we initially set the `alpha` variable to 0.95, the room will start out very dark, but not pitch-black but if you wish to start with the surface completely black, you can set `alpha` to 1. In order to create our "light switch," we tell GameMaker to check the value of `alpha` whenever we press the Spacebar key. If alpha is greater than 0, we set it to 0; otherwise, we set it back to `0.95`, our starting value. When we set `alpha` to 0, the surface's `alpha` value is also set to 0, making the instance of `darkSurface` completely translucent. This gives the impression that we've turned on the lights in the room as you can now see your player and all obstacles perfectly.

There's more

It's a best practice to play around with the alpha values in order to get the right feel for your lighting levels. There are very few instances in which you will find yourself in perfect darkness; there is always a light coming from somewhere. Because of this, it might not be a good idea to set your `alpha` levels to 1; instead, try various values between 0 and 1 until you get it right.

Lighting objects with a spot light

In the previous recipe, we were able to illuminate an entire room with a perfectly even light with the push of a button. In this case, that button was the spacebar and not an actual light switch, but you get the idea, right? Now, what if you don't want to light up the entire room at once? What if you want to shine a light on a smaller area, leaving the rest of the room in cold, scary darkness? Well, you're in luck! Let's take a look at how to create a mouse-controlled spotlight to investigate a dark scene.

Getting ready

We're going to continue from the scene that we created previously, so if you haven't finished it, now would be a good time. You'll also need a spot light sprite (spr_spotLight), which should be nothing more than a white circle and a spot light object (obj_spotLight, but *do not* assign the sprite to it).

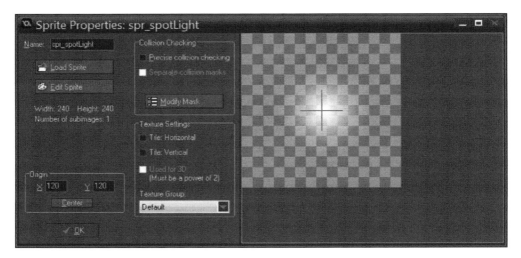

How to do it

1. Open obj_spotLight and add a **Create** event.

2. Drop a code block in the **Actions** box and enter the following code:

    ```
    lightStrength = 1;
    ```

3. Add a **Step** event and place a code block in the **Actions** box.

4. Enter the following code:

    ```
    x = mouse_x;
    y = mouse_y;
    ```

5. In obj_lightControl, open the code block in the **Draw** event.

6. Replace the code with the following code:

    ```
    surface_set_target(darkSurface);
    draw_clear(c_black);
    with(obj_spotLight)
    {
    ```

```
draw_set_blend_mode(bm_src_colour);
draw_sprite_ext(spr_spotLight, 0, x, y, image_xscale, image_
yscale, 0, c_white, lightStrength);
draw_set_blend_mode(bm_normal);
}
surface_reset_target();
draw_surface_ext(darkSurface, 0, 0, 1, 1, 0, c_white, alpha);
```

Place an instance of obj_spotLight in the room and you're all set. Test this recipe by moving the mouse around to see what you can find.

How it works

This recipe works like the previous one. In fact, the way in which we draw the initial surface is the same. Here, the real difference is that, before we reset the target surface to the screen, we add a new light source using obj_spotLight.

Correlating to the position of obj_spotLight (which correlates to the position of the mouse), we used draw_set_blend_mode(mode) and a sprite (spr_spotLight) to essentially create a window through the darkness of our surface. We did this by changing the blend mode to bm_src_color (it stands for *blend mode: source color*), which is one of the many blend modes provided by GameMaker. This worked in conjunction with the white circle represented in spr_spotLight to change the opacity of the darkened surface by blending the black and white colors, which is similar to the way in which we brightened the room in the previous recipe.

We then returned the blend mode to bm_normal before resetting the surface target.

You can get the same result using draw_circle_color(), but using a sprite you can have greater control over how the spotlight looks and blends. If you use a gradient circle (which I usually create using third-party software such as Photoshop), you can give your spotlight softer edges, making it much more realistic in terms of light diffusion.

There's more

Certain blending modes, including bm_src_color, will not work on specific platforms, namely, Android, iOS, Tizen, and HTML5 (without WebGL enabled). GameMaker offers several different blend modes for use in your projects. YoYo Games provides a visual explanation of how these blend modes work with shapes and sprites under draw_blend_mode_ext, which can be found at http://docs.yoyogames.com/.

Changing day to night

Though it has been done before, my first memory of a game with an active day/night cycle was *Legend of Zelda: Ocarina of Time*.

While running around most outdoor areas, the game's internal clock would cycle day to night and back to day again. Different enemies would appear between day and night, but the biggest change was to see how the world appeared. Enemies became less visible and the draw distance (how far you could see) was affected. Using what we've learned in this chapter so far, let's create a day/night cycle in GameMaker.

Getting ready

We'll start from scratch for this recipe because you only need three things: A room (`rm_game`), a block object to test your sight (`obj_block`), and a night cycle controller object (`obj_cycle`). Give `obj_block` a simple sprite and place it in random places around the room, but do not assign a sprite to `obj_cycle`. Also, make sure `obj_cycle` has a depth with a lower value than everything else in the room.

How to do it

1. In `obj_cycle`, add a **Create** event.

2. Drag a code block to the **Actions** box and enter the following code:

```
alpha = 0;
dayLength = 5;
nightLength = 3;
alarm[0] = room_speed*dayLength;
nightSurface = surface_create(room_width, room_height);
```

3. Add a **Draw** event to a code block.

4. Enter the following code:

```
surface_set_target(nightSurface);
draw_clear(c_black);
surface_reset_target();
draw_surface_ext(nightSurface, 0, 0, 1, 1, 0, c_white, alpha);
```

5. Add an event to `Alarm[0]` and place the following code in a code block:

```
if alpha < 0.95
{
alpha += 0.01;
```

```
alarm[0] = 1;
}
else if alpha >= 0.95
{
alarm[1] = room_speed*nightLength;
}
```

6. Repeat the previous step for an `Alarm[1]` event but replace the code with the following code:

```
if alpha > 0
{
alpha -= 0.01;
alarm[1] = 1;
}
else if alpha <= 0
{
alarm[0] = room_speed*dayLength;
}
```

Once these steps are complete, place an instance of `obj_cycle` in the room and test it out. Wait for at least five seconds to see the result.

How it works

The lighting elements of this recipe work like those of the first recipe in this chapter. We essentially cover everything in the room with an almost completely opaque black surface. This time, however, instead of changing the opacity of this sheet from one extreme to the other at the touch of a button, we allow timers to gradually change the surface's alpha, much like real life. The scene starts with an `alpha` value of 0, making the black surface completely transparent (daytime).

The `Alarm[0]` is set as the room speed (the framerate or number of steps per second) multiplied by the value of the `dayLength` variable. This, as the name plainly suggests, is how you decide how many seconds your day should last. We tested this out for 5 seconds. If you want your day to last for a minute, you should change this value to `60`.

Once `Alarm[0]` goes off, the code runs that adds `0.01` to the value of the `alpha` variable, which then sets `Alarm[0]` to 1, which means that in one step the same thing is going to happen: `0.01` will be added to the value of `alpha` and `Alarm[0]` will be reset to 1. This will repeat until `alpha` has a value of `0.95`.

At this point, the black surface will be almost completely opaque and GameMaker will stop setting `Alarm[0]` and set `Alarm[1]` to the room's speed multiplied by the value of `nightLength`.

Generally speaking, since nights are shorter than days in most parts of the world, this value will be less than `dayLength`. A similar cycle will be run with `0.01` being subtracted from the value of `alpha` until it reaches `0` and the cycle begins anew.

The best part of this recipe is the ease with which you can customize it. You can manage the day and night length by altering their respective values in the **Create** event. You can speed up or slow down the transition from day to night and back by altering the value added to or subtracted from alpha. You can also change how smoothly this transition takes place by changing the number of steps in both the alarms once the transition begins. In this recipe, we set this value to the lowest possible value (1) in order to create a smooth transition. I always recommend that you play around with all of these values until you find the best fit for your game's style.

There's more

This recipe deals with changing how much "light" we can see to mimic a day/night cycle. This isn't entirely realistic, as many changes take place when night falls. For instance, the sky takes the appearance of different colors when the sun is setting or rising. This can be mimicked by changing the background along with the timers already set in place.

In addition to this, you can also set different states during the night and day. Once alpha reaches a certain value (such as when night falls), you can change the ambient sounds (such as crickets chirping or owls hooting), or even have certain enemies spawn that wouldn't spawn during the day (just set a **Step** event that begins spawning those pesky skeletons once it's night time). There are many changes you can make here that are all based on the type of the game you're making, so go ahead and try something new!

Creating a flashlight

Even if you're not a fan of the genre, you need to be aware of the growing number of survival horror games on the market, especially the ones that are popular with indie developers. Many of these games (probably even *most* of them) require you to fumble around in dark, creepy locales as you attempt to solve a puzzle, unlock a secret, or find your long lost dad who disappeared under suspicious circumstances. What do the developers give you to aid you on your quest? A flashlight. One that keeps running out of batteries. Well, I have good news for you if you're looking to make a 2D survival horror game: we're going to learn how to create a flashlight effect in GameMaker.

Getting ready

Once again, you'll need a room (rm_game), a controllable player object (obj_player), an obstacle (obj_block), and a light controller object (obj_lightControl). Go ahead and place instances of obj_block around the room so that you can test them on completion. For this recipe, you'll also need a sprite to represent the flashlight's beam (spr_lightBeam). This sprite should resemble a cone of light that expands to the right with the size of your choice. Again, you can use a shape with solid lines if it suits your art style. I prefer a softer, more realistic light; for this, you would need to import an image (with the alpha layer intact) from third-party software, such as Photoshop.

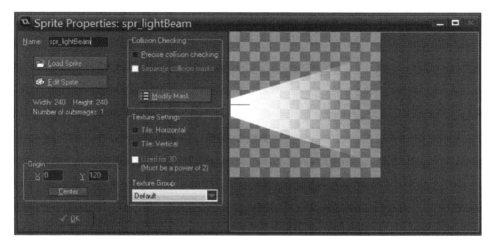

How to do it

1. In obj_lightControl, add a **Create** event.

2. Drop a code block in the **Actions** box and add the following code:
   ```
   alpha = 0.95;
   darkSurface = surface_create(room_width, room_height);
   ```

3. Add a **Draw** event.

4. Place a code block in the **Actions** box using the following code:
   ```
   surface_set_target(darkSurface);
   draw_clear(c_black);
   draw_set_blend_mode(bm_subtract);
   draw_sprite_ext(spr_lightBeam, 0, obj_player.x, obj_player.y, 1,
   1, dir, c_white, 1);
   ```

```
surface_reset_target();
draw_set_blend_mode(bm_normal);
draw_surface_ext(darkSurface, 0, 0, 1, 1, 0, c_black, alpha);
```

5. Add a **Step** event to a code block.

6. Enter the following code:

```
dir = point_direction(obj_player.x, obj_player.y, mouse_x,
mouse_y);
```

Once these steps are complete, place an instance each of `obj_lightControl` and `obj_player` in the room and test them out. Move your character around the room and use your mouse to shine your flashlight.

How it works

As with the other recipes in this chapter, we're creating a black surface, then making this surface transparent to the desired degree. As discussed in the spotlight recipe, we're not affecting the entire surface, but rather a small portion of it—specifically the shape of our flashlight beam.

The difference here is the blend mode we're using. Previously, we used `bm_src_colour` to subtract the color of our sprite (white) from the color of the surface (black).

With `bm_subtract`, the shape of the sprite you create is subtracted from the surface to which it is applied, not unlike a cut-out. Any transparencies in the sprite are not cut out so, by changing the alpha level of the sprite, you're increasing the opacity of the area that you are otherwise trying to make translucent.

This is great for creating a flashlight effect using images that are imported with alpha layers. Light from a flashlight isn't perfectly distributed; with most flashlight types, there is an intense beam with a narrow field and far reach coupled with a wider spread light that doesn't reach as far.

Using a layered image (with the intense beam as the top layer) and keeping transparencies intact when exporting, you can have a sprite with two different opacities.

If you're going for more realism, make the wide angle light much softer and make the tip of the intense beam soft and round.

If you take a look at the values set in `draw_sprite_ext()`, you'll notice a couple of things. First, you'll notice that the x and y coordinates of our light beam sprite are set to those of `obj_player`. This is, as I'm sure you guessed, to have the light beam follow our player, giving the illusion of the player carrying a flashlight. Second, you may have noticed that we declare the `dir` variable in the **Step** event and call it when we draw our sprite.

Here, we're setting the sprite's rotation to be constantly updated using `point_direction()` so that the flashlight is always pointing toward the mouse. This creates an intuitively controlled light beam; you point your mouse to whatever you'd like to illuminate.

Now, one important thing I have to mention here is that it's imperative that you reset the blend mode back to `bm_normal` once the light beam sprite has been drawn. This prevents any undesired effects, whereby other images are blended incorrectly.

Making a flickering torch

Flashlights are all well and good but sometimes you need to go for a classic. That's where the torch comes in; a staple of dungeons and thatched-roof cottages alike. What's the main difference between a torch and flashlight? Besides the technology, a torch has a dynamic light source: fire.

As a fire burns, the flames seem to dance about, seemingly casting a moving light. In this recipe, we're going to see a simple way to mimic this effect.

Getting ready

Let's start with the project from a previous recipe from this chapter: changing day to night. We're going to add a torch object (`obj_torch`) and you'll want to give it an appropriate sprite with an animated flame (`spr_torch`). Most importantly, you'll need a second sprite to represent the light given out by the torch (`spr_torchLight`). This sprite looks best as a circular gradient, going from transparent to white. Make sure you place instances of `obj_torch` around the room.

How to do it

1. In `obj_cycle`, open the **Draw** event.
2. Make some space right after the `draw_clear(c_black)` code. If you exactly follow the original recipe, this space should begin on line 3.
3. Enter the following code:

```
with(obj_torch)
{
    draw_set_blend_mode(bm_subtract);
    draw_sprite_ext(spr_torchLight, 0, x, y, lightSize, lightSize,
0, c_white, 1);
    draw_set_blend_mode(bm_normal);
}
```

4. In `obj_torch`, add a **Create** event.

5. Drag a code block to the **Actions** box and enter the following code:

    ```
    image_speed = 0.4;
    lightSize = 1;
    ```

6. Add a **Step** event to a code block.

7. Enter the following code:

    ```
    flicker = choose(0.01, -0.01, 0);
    lightSize += flicker;
    lightsize = clamp(lightSize, 0.95, 1.15);
    ```

Once this is complete, you are free to test it. Make sure to play around with the values in the **Step** event of `obj_torch` until you get the flicker effect you desire.

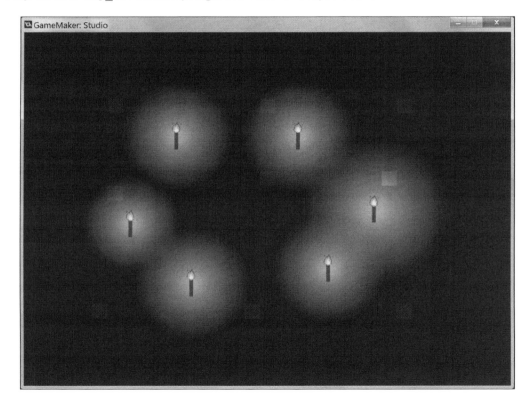

How it works

Once again, we used the `bm_subtract` blend mode to add the torch light to our scene. Since the light is drawn directly on top of the torch itself, it appears as though the torch is cutting through the darkness. The flicker gives the effect that the fire of the torch is really burning.

This is accomplished by allowing GameMaker to choose one of the three values (`0.01`, `-0.01`, or `0`) and adding it to the value of the `lightSize` variable, which is used to determine the size of the sprite (a value of `1` means the sprite is exactly the same size as it was when you first created it).

One thing to note here is the use of the `clamp()` function. The `clamp()` function is used to control the range of the given value.

In our case, we used `clamp()` to ensure that the `lightSize` variable didn't get any smaller than 0.85 times its original size and didn't grow beyond 1.15 times its original size. Without this function, adding and subtracting the value of the flicker from `lightSize` could cause it to shrink down to nothing or grow larger than the room itself.

As I mentioned earlier, it's best if you play around with these values until the flicker effect works the way you want it to.

9

Particle Man, Particle Man – Adding Polish to Your Game with Visual Effects and Particles

In this chapter, we'll cover the following recipes:

- ▶ Using particles to simulate kicking up dust
- ▶ Simulating rainfall
- ▶ Creating an explosion
- ▶ Adding screen-shake
- ▶ Using slow motion

Introduction

In this book, so far, we've seen quite a bit of what you can do to make a game using GameMaker. Each of the recipes in the previous chapters can be followed to create an element of a game, be it the control scheme, sound system, or interface element. If you put these elements together, you will get a game.

Well, technically, it's a game, but the question you should be asking is "Is it fun?" There's a major component of game design that isn't always obvious and that many (including myself) have taken to calling "game feel."

Game feel refers mostly to (often) minor elements of a game that contribute to the fun of playing. This could be anything to do with controlling the game (response time), any type of feedback (visual or audio cues related to game progression), or any number of other aspects related to engaging the player. Game feel, to me, is any element that adds excitement to the game; it's what draws you in and keeps you there, immersed in the gameplay. If you've ever played games by developers such as Capy Games or Vlambeer, you know what I'm talking about. These developers and others have mastered the art of driving a gameplay with frenetic, flashy effects that enthrall rather than distract. In this recipe, we'll take a look at how to create effects that keep players thinking about a game long after they've put down the controller.

Particles

When referring to visual effects in a game, particles are often the heart of the discussion. Particles can be used to create anything from weather (rain) to clouds (smoke, dust, and so on) to explosions (fire and sparks). GameMaker has a handful of built-in particle effects to speak of, but you can also customize them to fit your vision. Here, we'll take a look at the various uses of particles, the bread and butter of visual effects in games.

- ▶ Using particles to simulate kicking up dust
- ▶ Simulating rainfall
- ▶ Creating an explosion

Game feedback

There's nothing as satisfying as a game that properly telegraphs what's happening on screen. Some games will play corresponding sounds (as we discussed in *Chapter 5, Now Hear This! – Music and Sound Effects*) but others will go the extra mile and throw in some excellent visual cues as well. You might take these elements for granted when playing yourself, but the following section will show you how to implement an important game feedback that will draw the player into your game.

- ▶ Adding screen-shake
- ▶ Using slow motion

Using particles to simulate kicking up dust

Even if your game's art style isn't meant to be photorealistic, there are many subtle things you can do to make them more immersive. One such thing is to add environmental cues, such as dust clouds, where your player character moves. Have you ever run down a dirt road? If so, your feet have certainly kicked up quite a bit of dust as you travelled along. Let's add the same effect to your game to give more depth to the environment.

Getting ready

To start with, you'll need the following objects: two separate ground parent objects (`obj_grndParent_norm` and `obj_grndParent_dirt`), two separate ground objects (`obj_ground_norm` and `obj_ground_dirt`), and a player object (`obj_player`). Give the two ground objects different sprites and assign their respective parent objects, as we did in *Chapter 2, It's Under Control – Exploring Various Control Schemes*. Set up a room with a long platform consisting of sections of each type of ground object so that we can see the difference between running over one versus the other when testing. Once this is complete, we're ready to begin.

How to do it...

1. In `obj_player`, add a **Step** event.

2. Drag two code blocks to the **Actions** box.

3. In the first block, add the following code:

```
if keyboard_check(vk_right)
{
    hspeed = 10;
}
else if keyboard_check(vk_left)
{
    hspeed = -10;
}
else
{
    hspeed = 0;
}
```

4. In the second block, add the following code:

```
if !place_meeting(x, y, obj_groundParent_norm) && !place_
meeting(x, y, obj_groundParent_dirt)
{
    vspeed = 5;
}
else
{
```

```
        vspeed = 0;
}

if place_meeting(x, y, obj_groundParent_dirt) && (hspeed > 0)
{
    effect_create_below(ef_smoke, x, y+8, 0, c_white);
}
else if place_meeting(x, y, obj_groundParent_dirt) && (hspeed < 0)
{
    effect_create_below(ef_smoke, x, y+8, 0, c_white);
}
```

Once these steps are complete, add an instance of `obj_player` anywhere above the ground objects in the room and you're ready to test it. Use the right and left arrow keys to allow the player run back and forth across the different types of grounds and watch the dust fly.

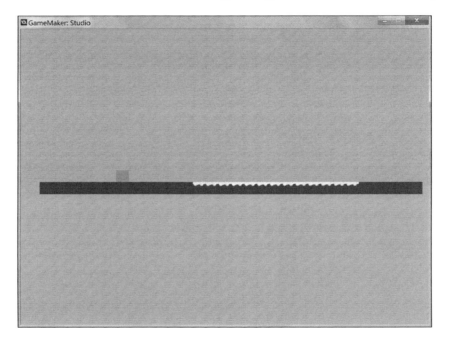

And then it looks like this:

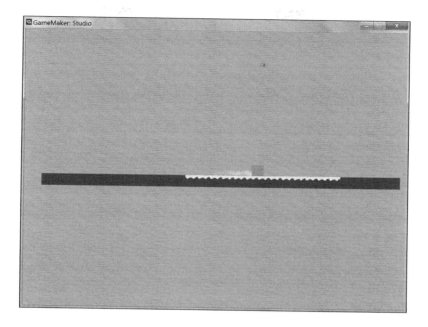

How it works...

This recipe introduces you to one of GameMaker's built-in particle effects, namely, ef_smoke. This effect, along with the other 11 effects (which YoYo Games refers to as *Simple Effects*), requires little to incorporate them into your game.

Here, we used the effect_create_below() function that, as the name suggests, creates an instance of the particle *below* the object housing the code. GameMaker will repeat this for every step as long as it is told to do so. We instruct GameMaker to create an instance for each step, so as long as the player moves it is in contact with obj_grndParent_dirt. (This is especially useful because it is unlikely you'll want your player's footfalls to kick up dust *all* of the time.)

Using the requested parameters, we set the coordinates to reflect those of the player object, but we add eight pixels to the *y* coordinate to make it seem as though the clouds are coming from the player's feet. We also set the size as the default size and set the colour to c_white. The default size (0) is the smallest size required to make the particles, but you can make them larger by setting this value to 1 or 2.

There's more...

If you want to make this a little more fun, try playing around with the simple effects you use. Instead of `ef_smoke`, try `ef_ring`, `ef_firework`, or `ef_star`, play around with the particle type, color, and size until you find something that fits your game's style.

Simulating rainfall

One thing I enjoy is when a game developer adds some small touches to increase the player's immersion in the game's world. How can you go about doing this? Why not add some real-world elements to start with? Let's try making it rain. By this, I mean simulating drops of water falling from the sky, not tossing dollar bills in slow motion; though this would also be cool.

Getting ready

The following recipe is incredibly easy and illustrates another way in which you can use GameMaker's built-in simple particle effects. We're going to continue from the scene that we created in the previous recipe, and we only need to add one thing: a rainmaker object called `obj_rain`. Seems simple enough, right? Let's take a look at how it can work.

How to do it...

1. In `obj_rain`, add a **Step** event.
2. Drag a code block to the **Actions** box and add the following code:
    ```
    effect_create_above(ef_rain, 0, 0, 0, c_white);
    ```
3. Place an instance of `obj_rain` anywhere in the room.

That's it! Once these steps have been completed, go ahead and test it out.

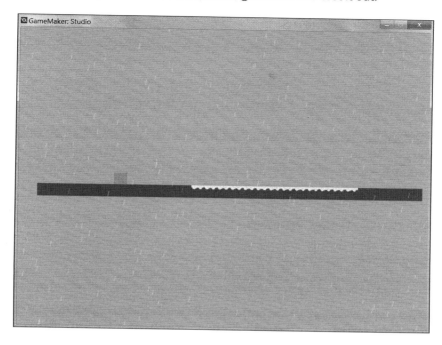

How it works...

As I mentioned earlier, this recipe was simply used to demonstrate the second form of GameMaker's simple effects. Here, we used `effect_create_above()` to create the selected effect *above* all the other objects in the room.

Now, if you were to run this effect once, it would create a few drops of rain. Since we added this code to a **Step** event, however, it is repeated for every step until we tell it to stop. The arguments in this function work just as they do with `effect_create_below`, but since we are using `ef_rain` for our effect, there are some minor changes. Firstly, the *x* and *y* coordinates (that we set to 0, 0) are inconsequential. With `ef_rain`, no matter where you place them in the room or what coordinates you provide, the rain will always have the default settings of the top-left corner of the room (0, 0). This is to ensure that the rain particles fall across the entire room and do not begin abruptly in one place or another.

Secondly, the argument that deals with the size of the particle does not affect the size of the individual rain drops. Instead, changing the value from 0 to 2 will alter the frequency at which the drops fall. Do you want heavier rain? Then, you need to change this value.

Unfortunately, it's not possible to change the speed of the rainfall or the size of the drops of water. However, it is possible to add some depth. What I would like to do is add a *second* line of code to the Step event, thereby creating a second instance of the rain particles. Below the first line, I add the following code:

```
effect_create_below(ef_rain, 0, 0, 0, c_gray);
```

By adding a second rainfall *behind* everything and with a darker color, we can add depth to the scene by creating the illusion of the rain falling from a distance.

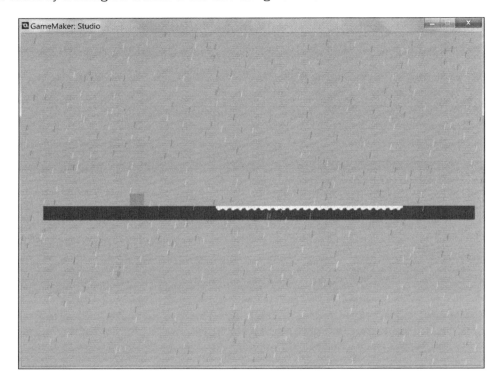

There's more...

If you're interested in creating weather in a colder climate, using `ef_snow` in place of `ef_rain` is the way to go. This effect will provide snowflakes of varying sizes that float downward slowly in a randomized pattern instead of downward in a straight line. Once again, by creating two instances, one above and one below, you can add more depth to the weather effect and increase the immersion in the game world.

Creating an explosion

What kind of a game doesn't have any explosions? Well, I'm sure there are *some* out there, but do you really want to play them? I doubt it* and that's why we're going to learn a little bit about GameMaker's particle systems by creating explosions. This will be much more coding-intensive than our previous forays into particles but, once we're done, you'll have plenty to play around with. GameMaker's particle systems and particle emitters can make some pretty interesting effects that add a lot of polish with just a little effort.

*I don't actually doubt it but just go with it.

Getting ready

We're going to start from scratch for this recipe. Due to the colors we'll be using and the nature of the recipe, I recommend that you change the background color of the room that you set to black. You'll also need two objects: `obj_control` (our controller object) and `obj_partEmit_exp` (our particle emitter object). Place an instance of `obj_control` in the room.

How to do it...

1. In `obj_control`, add a **Step** event.
2. Place a code block in the **Actions** box and enter the following code:

```
if mouse_check_button_pressed(mb_left)
{
    instance_create(mouse_x, mouse_y, obj_partEmit_exp);
}
```

3. In `obj_partEmit_exp`, add a **Create** event to a code block.
4. Enter the following code:

```
alarm[0] = room_speed*3;

partExp_sys = part_system_create();

partExp = part_type_create();
part_type_shape(partExp, pt_shape_explosion);
part_type_size(partExp, 0.8, 1, -0.01, 0);
part_type_scale(partExp, 1, 1);
part_type_speed(partExp, 1, 1, 0, 0);
part_type_direction(partExp, 0, 359, 0, 0);
part_type_gravity(partExp, 0.05, 90);
part_type_colour3(partExp, c_red, c_orange, c_white);
part_type_alpha3(partExp, 0.5, 1, 0.75);
```

```
part_type_blend(partExp, true);
part_type_life(partExp, room_speed, room_speed*2);

partExp_emit = part_emitter_create(partExp_sys);
part_emitter_region(partExp_sys, partExp_emit, x-80, x+80, y-60,
y+60, ps_shape_ellipse, ps_distr_linear);
part_emitter_burst(partExp_sys, partExp_emit, partExp, 50 +
irandom(30));
```

5. Add an event to `Alarm[0]`.

6. Drag a code block to the **Actions** box and add the following code:

```
instance_destroy();
```

7. Add a **Destroy** event to a code block.

8. Enter the following code:

```
part_system_destroy(partExp_sys);
```

Once these steps are complete, you are free to test your particle system. Run the program and try clicking on the room.

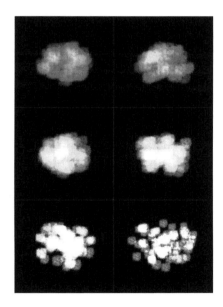

Don't quite like the results? Keep reading to find out how it works so that you can fine-tune what you've created.

How it works...

The first piece of code is pretty self-explanatory: all it does is create an instance of our particle emitter object (not the emitter itself) whenever we click on the left mouse button. The real magic happens within the emitter object itself and is complex in terms of how much code is necessary, but satisfying in how easy it is to customize your particles once the code is in place.

We're going to break this code down line by line in order to see how GameMaker's particles work.

The first line allows us to keep the time in check regardless of the room's speed; one second will be equal to one second whether you're running at 30, 60, or more steps/second.

Moving on, the next line is one of *the* most important lines. This is where you can set up the particle system that will allow you to create the particles themselves as well as the emitter that will use them. You'll need to insert it in any object where you wish to create particles. Here, you'll name your particle system any way you wish. I've named this one `partExp_sys` so that, when I need to debug it, I know that this is a particle system for an explosion effect and this variable refers to the overall system. Normally, I would type out the full name (to make everything transparent in terms of function) but, as you can see, the variables must be typed out *several* times. This naming convention allows you to label it properly without making it too long-winded.

Next, we give our individual particles a name by creating the `partExp` variable (again, it is short yet descriptive) and assigning it the `part_type_create()` function, which does exactly what it says and creates a new particle type. This must be done before we define the particles because, without this line of code, GameMaker has no point of reference.

From here, we get into the attributes of our particles. This list (which I will describe line by line) represents some, but not all, of the options you have when creating particles. The attributes I've chosen here allow me to have the particles look and act how I want them to. Let's take a look at what we used to describe our explosion particles. Keep in mind that the order of the code is important here.

> ▶ `part_type_shape(index, shape)`: This line describes the shape the particles have to take. Here, we instruct GameMaker as to the index of the particle we wish to use (`partExp`) as well as which particle we choose from the list of 14 built-in particles (`pt_shape_explosion`). If you do not wish to use a particle from this list, you can use `part_type_sprite` in order to use a sprite of your choice. With this function, you can even customize how the animation can be displayed.
>
> Once the shape (or sprite) has been selected, we can move on to describe how the particles should look and act.

► `part_type_size(index, minimum, maximum, increase, wiggle)`: Getting the particle size values is very important. Here, we set the particle's minimum start size, maximum start size, and how much the size changes with each step of the particle's life, as well as how much can be randomly added or subtracted from the particle's size per step. We set different values for the minimum and maximum, which means the particles will begin their lives at random sizes within these parameters. We set a negative value for the increase, which means our particles will shrink a little bit at each step. When coding this, I only wanted the particles to shrink, not fluctuate in size. For this reason, the wiggle is set to `0`.

► `part_type_scale(index, xscale, yscale)`: Setting the particle's scale is straightforward, but you should note that you can set the scale of *x* and *y* separately.

► `part_type_speed(index, minimum start speed, maximum start speed, increase, wiggle)`: The speed at which your particles travel is paramount, so you'll find yourself using this function every time. With `part_type_speed`, you can set the minimum and maximum speed values at which your particles can begin their lives. You can then instruct GameMaker to change this speed incrementally with each step, be it increasing the speed (positive number) or slowing it down (negative number). You can also change the speed randomly using wiggle. This value will be added or subtracted with every step.

► `part_type_direction(index, minimum direction, maximum directions, increase, wiggle)`: This function works in a similar way to `part_type_speed`. Here, instead of setting your particle's speed, you're setting your particle's direction in terms of degrees. As we discussed in the previous chapters, GameMaker reads the direction in 360 degrees beginning with `0` degrees as right and going counter-clockwise from there. We want our particles to travel every which way (explosions radiate outwards), so the starting direction of our particles is anywhere between 0 to 359 degrees (a full circle). The particles can also change the direction at every step by adding a positive or negative value to the increase argument. This will cause the value you entered to be added to the particle's current direction at every step, causing it to move in a circle. By adding a value to the wiggle argument, you can change the direction randomly as this value will be added to the particle's direction in conjunction with any value added by the increase argument. We set both of these values to `0`, which means that our particles will not change direction at each step.

► `part_type_gravity(index, gravity strength, and gravity direction)`: Adding gravity to your particles isn't necessary, but it does make some interesting effects. With this function, you can set the strength of the gravity (a effecting only the indexed particles) and from which direction it can pull your particles. Our particles are being affected by a very slight gravitational pull (0.05) coming from above (90 degrees, in line with GameMaker's direction). This gives the illusion of the explosion dissipating and turning into clouds of smoke; they begin to gently float up.

- `part_type_colour3(index, 1st color, 2nd color, and 3rd color)`: This is one of the several options used for setting the color of your particles. This function will have your particles begin their lives as the 1st color and transition to the 2nd and 3rd colors at the halfway point and end of their lives, respectively. Using `part_type_colour2` will do the same with only two colors, while `part_type_colour1` has the particles sticking to the color of your choice throughout. You can also use `part_type_colour_mix` to blend selected colors but, if you really want control over the display colors and transitions of your particles, I suggest that you try `part_type_colour_rgb` or `part_type_colour_hsv`. These functions allow you to set the minimum and maximum numbers for RGB (red, green, and blue) or HSV (hue, saturation, and value), depending on which one you choose.

- `part_type_alpha3(index, 1st alpha, 2nd alpha, and 3rd alpha)`: This function works just like `part_type_colour3`. Here, instead of a color, you need to choose the alpha values for the beginning, middle, and end stages of your particle's life.

- `part_type_blend(index, additive blending)`: This function dictates whether your particles will be drawn or not using additive blending. Additive blending will add together the luminosity of overlapping particles, making light colors brighter (until white) and darker colors more transparent (until black). This is perfect for our explosion effect, as areas with a higher concentration of particles will make the display much brighter, giving the illusion of a greater intensity. For this reason, we set the additive blending value to `true`.

- `part_type_life(index, minimum lifespan, and maximum lifespan)`: The `part_type_life` function does exactly what you think it does. Using this function, we can instruct GameMaker to decide each particle's lifespan in terms of steps. You can have all your particles last for the same length of time by setting the same value for the minimum and maximum lifespan, or you can set different values and have GameMaker choose a random number between them. In order to allow our particles to live between one and two seconds, no matter what the room speed is, our minimum and maximum values are set to the room speed or the room speed is multiplied by 2.

Once we've instructed GameMaker on the look and actions we wish our particles to assume, we must provide the means for them to be created in-game. Enter the particle emitter. Particle emitters do exactly as their name suggests; they emit particles. Before our emitter can do so, however, we must provide GameMaker with an adequate description as to how it should go about doing its duties.

First, we must place the emitter in a variable. To do this, we use `part_emitter_create`. With this function, the emitter will be created within the particle system that we provide as an argument (in our case, `partExp_sys`) and will therefore be able to work within the system's parameters.

Next, we need to set the area in which the emitter can display particles. This is important as your particles will serve a specific purpose and must be displayed appropriately. In order to do so, we use the `part_emitter_region` function (a particle system, index, x minimum, x maximum, y minimum, y maximum, region shape, and particle distribution). This function is vital to how your system is displayed. Setting the x and y minimum and maximum values sets the region in which the particle emitter works. It does this in conjunction with the particle region shape. By setting the region shape to `ps_shape_ellipse`, we're giving our particles a round area in which they can be displayed (a rectangle, diamond, and line being the other options). The x and y values that precede this argument provide the coordinates and ranges for this elliptical shape. In our case, wherever you click the mouse, that's where the emitter will be placed. From there, the particles can be displayed 80 pixels to the left and right of the center of the object, and 60 pixels above and below it.

Within this area, we need to also specify how the particles will be distributed. We're using `ps_distr_gaussian`, which concentrates the majority of the particles in the center. We could also have chosen `ps_distr_invgaussian` (particles concentrated on region edges) or `ps_distr_linear` (particles distributed evenly throughout), but the Gaussian distribution works best for an explosion effect.

Finally, we must provide instructions for how our particles will be emitted. For this, there are two options: `part_emitter_burst` and `part_emitter_stream`. The latter will provide a constant stream of particles for which you need to provide the number of particles you create at each step. The former, the one that we've chosen, emits a set number of particles but only once. In order to make each explosion unique, we've set the emitter to burst 50 particles plus a random number of particles from 1 to 30.

This takes care of the creation and display of our particle system, but there's one more extremely important thing to do. Whenever you create a particle system, it sticks around until you remove it. This means that, even if you move to another room or to the end of the game, the particle system remains. If you leave this as is, it can lead to memory leaks and even crash your game. To prevent this, we must destroy the particle system, thereby removing it from memory. This can be done in many ways, such as when an enemy is destroyed, when a room ends, or when the player quits or restarts the game. In our case, we used an Alarm event to kill our particle system. When an instance of `obj_partEmit_exp` is created, the first thing it does is set an alarm to count down from 3 seconds (`room_speed*3`). This allows more than enough time for each and every particle created to run its lifespan (which is, at most, 2 seconds). When this alarm goes off, the object is destroyed. As it is destroyed, the **Destroy** event runs the `part_system_destroy` function. This destroys whichever particle system is indexed in the argument (since you can have more than one particle system in place at once). With the particle system destroyed, it is no longer a drain on the memory and you can avoid nasty memory leaks.

As long-winded as this explanation is, it is important to understand that particle systems are technically complex but can be straightforward when you understand your options. As with many elements of GameMaker, I highly recommend that you play around with values and variables if you want, to see what you can create.

Despite the number of functions described in this recipe, there are actually many more to see. Make sure that you check out all of the information on particles, available at `http://docs.yoyogames.com/`.

Adding screen-shake

One of my favorite effects, screen-shake, is a great way to add some depth and excitement to your game. As you may have guessed, I'm referring to the visual effects of making the screen-shake in order to simulate the effect of a shock or impact. Game developers, Vlambeer, know how to add excitement to games, such as *Luftrausers* and *Nuclear Throne*, by correlating the action with screen-shake; if you get hit or an explosion goes off, you'll know it. Let's see how we can add screen-shake using GameMaker.

Getting ready

Screen-shake often takes place when an explosion occurs on screen, making this recipe a perfect follow up to the previous one. Let's add on to the particle recipe using the same project file. In order to show off the effect, you'll need to add some visible objects to the background. This will allow you to see the screen moving back and forth. I added several instances of `obj_block`, which has a simple 32 x 32 square for its sprite. There's no need to make changes to the particle object; we'll be working solely with `obj_control`. We will, however, need to make use of views within the room, so let's start.

How to do it...

1. In your room, click on the **Views** tab and make sure **Enable the use of views** is checked.
2. Check the box next to **Visible when room starts**.
3. Under **View in room** and **Port on screen**, set the w and h values to `640` and `480`, respectively. This is based on the default room size of `1024` by `768`. Keep the x and y values as `0`.
4. Based on the preview of your new view, place instances of `obj_block` around the visible area.
5. In `obj_control`, add a **Create** event.
6. Place a code block in the **Actions** box and enter the following code:

    ```
    shake = false;
    ```

7. Open the code block located in the **Step** event.

8. Within the code for the **Left Mouse Button** check, add the following code:

```
shake = true;
alarm[0] = room_speed*0.8;
```

9. After the **Left Mouse Button** code, enter the following code:

```
if shake
{
    view_xview[0] = random_range(-5, 5);
    view_yview[0] = random_range(-5, 5);
}
```

10. Add an event to `Alarm[0]` and place a code block in the **Actions** box.

11. Enter the following code:

```
shake = false;
view_xview[0] = 0;
view_yview[0] = 0;
```

You can now test your new and improved explosion effect with the combined power of particles and screen-shake.

How it works...

This method of creating screen-shake effect is fairly straightforward. Using views, we don't have to worry about moving anything within the room (which would be incredibly costly, memory-wise), we just have to move what is essentially a rudimentary camera.

If you've ever seen an episode of Star Trek, you know that when the ship is hit everyone in the scene is shaken. What really happens that is the actors move as though they're in an earthquake zone while the camera man shakes the camera back and forth to make it more believable. What we've done here isn't much different. Views allow you to present an area on screen that is smaller than the room itself. If you were to make a large platformer level and test it without views, you would see the entire level all at once and your player character would be miniscule. To get around this, you need to use views in order to shrink the viewable area while maintaining the room itself. In the **Views** tab of the room editor, we can do this by setting the viewable area to 640 x 480 while the room itself is set at 1024 x 768.

The difference between **View in room** and **Port on screen** is that the former dictates the viewable area while the latter dictates the resolution at which it is displayed. If you set the **View in room** to 640 x 480 in a 1024 x 768 room, an area of 640 x 480 would be visible and the rest would be cut off. If you were to then set the **Port on screen** values to 320 x 240, the same area would be viewable but it would be displayed at a resolution of 320 x 240.

To shake the screen, we had to create a new `shake` variable. When we click on the left mouse button, an instance of the particle object (explosion) is created. Since we want the screen to shake when the explosion takes place, we set `shake` to true and set an alarm. The length of the alarm represents how long the `shake` variable will remain `true` and therefore how long the screen will shake. Next, we instructed GameMaker to follow some instructions while `shake` is `true`. In order to make the screen appear to shake, GameMaker can change the x and y origins of the `view[0]`. We can accomplish this by changing `view_xview[0]` and `view_yview[0]` to a random value within the range of `-5` to `5`. This happens at every step. The result is the viewport jumping around within 5 pixels in any direction for a period of less than a second. At the end of this period (the length of time it takes the alarm to count down), shake once again becomes `false` and the view is returned to its original x and y coordinates of `0`.

Using slow motion

John Woo had it right: slow motion makes things look way cooler. Well, as far as action goes, anyway. How many games since the late 90s have made use of slow motion in one way or another? It often comes in the form of some kind of power up or usage meter, but it's there and it's a lot of fun. Do you want to add slow motion to your game? Let's take a look at one way in which you can accomplish this using GameMaker.

Getting ready

To make things simpler, we'll continue to use the project file from the two previous recipes. In addition to this, who doesn't want to see explosions in slow motion? You won't need to create any new objects here, but we'll be working with `obj_control`.

How to do it...

1. In the **Create** event of `obj_control`, add the following code:
   ```
   globalvar timeSpeed;
   globalvar slowMo;
   slowMo = false;
   timeSpeed = 1;
   ```

2. In the **Step** event, add the following code *before* the first line of code:
   ```
   room_speed = round(60*timeSpeed);
   ```

3. In the same code block, add the following code *after* the existing code:
   ```
   if keyboard_check_pressed(vk_space)
   {
       if slowMo == false
       {       slowMo = true;
       }
       else
       {
           slowMo = false;
       }
   }
   ```

4. Add a new code block to the same **Step** event.

5. Enter the following code:

```
if slowMo == true
{
    if (timeSpeed > 0.2)
    {
        timeSpeed -= 0.05;
    }
    else
    {
        timeSpeed = 0.2;
    }
}
else
{
    if (timeSpeed < 1)
    {
        timeSpeed += 0.05;
    }
    else
    {
        timeSpeed = 1;
    }
}
```

You are now ready to experience basic slow motion effects. You can turn slow motion on and off by pressing the Spacebar key.

How it works...

This recipe uses some shortcuts but demonstrates the basic theory behind slowing down the time in your game. Everything in your game uses the room speed to determine timing. By changing the room speed, we can control this timing by slowing the game down (as we've done here) or even speeding things up. Now, you'll notice that we've altered the room speed using `room_speed = round equation (60*timeSpeed)`. This means that we are setting the room speed using the code (instead of leaving that to a value in the room editor).

We do this by finding the nearest integer when multiplying 60 (our desired normal room speed) by the value of `timeSpeed`. When the spacebar is pressed, the `slowMo` variable is either turned on or turned off. If `slowMo` becomes `true`, the value of `timeSpeed` drops by `0.05` every step until it reaches `0.2`. It stays at this value until `slowMo` is turned off again, at which point the value of `timeSpeed` is increased by `0.05` every step until it reaches the default value we set, which is `1`.

At its slowest, the room speed becomes 12 steps per second, which means that the time passes at 1/5th the speed it normally does.

There's more...

As I mentioned earlier, this is one way of achieving the effect of slow motion. Another way is to alter individual properties, such as the movement speed and timers. This allows greater customization and different objects to operate at different speeds. While this would be accomplished in the same way as the preceding recipe, it could be a far more daunting task to code and debug, depending on the number and complexity of particles, as you would need to alter one or more variables for each object affected by the time change.

10
Hello, World – Creating New Dimensions of Play Through Networking

In this recipe, we'll cover the following topics:

- ▶ Basic networks
- ▶ Asynchronous play

Introduction

Today's multiplayer experiences fall into two main categories: real-time online and asynchronous online play. Gone are the days of sitting on the couch with your friends as you beat each other up on screen. This statement isn't entirely accurate with games, such as *Super Smash Bros*, which proves the exception to the rule, but there is an obvious trend toward an online play. Many primarily single-player games are being augmented with multiplayer game modes, while many others, such as multiplayer online battle arena games, for example, *League of Legends*, are strictly online multiplayer games with no single-player campaigns. To give you some idea of where this trend is going, Riot Games (whose only developed games as of 2015 is *League of Legends*) generated $624 million USD in 2013 and was poised to break the $1 billion (with a "B") USD mark in 2014. This is solely from micro transactions, as the game is primarily free to play. Clearly, having online gameplay makes up for a lot of time invested by players all over the world. Keeping this in mind, let's take a look at how GameMaker handles online play.

Basic networking

You must learn to walk before you can run. Similarly, you must learn to connect before you can play online. This section will teach you the basics of creating a network using GameMaker.

- ▸ Connecting a client to a server

Online play

Here, we'll take a look at one type of online play: asynchronous turn-based play. Just like in video games, this style appears in real life. Consider playing football versus playing chess. In football, everyone on the field is playing simultaneously; there is no waiting involved, except between plays, when everyone is waiting. This is synchronous play. Conversely, in chess, after you make a decision and move a piece on the board, you cannot do so again until your opponent has done the same. You can survey the board and devise your strategy, but until it is your turn once again, you cannot play. This is asynchronous play. Using our newfound knowledge of networking, let's use GameMaker to simulate some turn-based play.

- ▸ Setting up asynchronous play for a turn-based game

Connecting a client to a server

In order to play a game online, you must first connect to other players. In the early days of computer gaming, this was done with a direct connection from one computer to another. These days, it is far more common for all players involved to connect to a server in order to enjoy multiplayer games. Let's take a look at how to create a server/client relationship using GameMaker.

Getting ready

Since we're going to learn how to connect a client to a server, we're going to need both a client *and* server. For this purpose, you'll need two different projects open at one time: `network_test_server.gmx` and `network_test_client.gmx`, each with a single room. You'll need to create specific objects *during* this tutorial instead of in preparation for it, so make sure you pay attention to the project file you're working with at all times.

How to do it...

1. In `network_test_server.gmx`, create an object called `obj_server`.
2. Add a **Create** event and drag a code block to the **Actions** box.

3. Enter the following code:

```
server = network_create_server(network_socket_tcp, 9001, 8);
socket = noone;
```

4. Add a **Networking** event, which is found under **Asynchronous**.

5. Place a code block in the **Actions** box and add the following code:

```
typeEvent = async_load[? "type"];
switch (typeEvent)
{
    case network_type_connect:
    if (socket == noone)
    {
        socket = async_load[? "socket"];
    }
    break;

    case network_type_disconnect:
    socket = noone;
    break;

    case network_type_data:
    buffer = async_load[? "buffer"];
    buffer_seek (buffer, buffer_seek_start, 0);
    scr_packetReceive (buffer);
    break;
}
```

6. Add a **Game End** event, which is found under **Other**.

7. Add a code block and enter the following code:

```
network_destroy(server);
```

8. Create an object called `obj_signal` and add a **Draw** event.

9. Add a code block containing the following code:

```
draw_text(x, y, "Hello, world.");
```

10. Create a script called `scr_packetReceive` and enter the following code:

```
buffer = argument[0];
message_id = buffer_read(buffer, buffer_u8);
switch(message_id)
{
    case 1:
```

```
instance_create(random(room_width),random(room_height), obj_
signal);
    break;
}
```

11. Place an instance of `obj_server` anywhere in the room.

12. In `network_test_client.gmx`, create an object called `obj_client`.

13. Add a **Create** event and place a code block in the **Actions** box.

14. Enter the following code:

```
ip = "xxx.xxx.x.xxx"; //Replace with your own IP address
socket = network_create_socket(network_socket_tcp);
connect = network_connect(socket, ip, 9001);
buffer = buffer_create(1024, buffer_fixed, 1);
```

15. Add a **Game End** event.

16. Place a code block in the **Actions** box and enter the following code:

```
network_destroy(socket);
buffer_delete(buffer);
```

17. Create an object called `obj_button` and add a **Left Mouse Button Pressed** event.

18. Place a code block in the **Actions** box and enter the following code:

```
with(obj_client)
{
buffer_seek(buffer, buffer_seek_start, 0);
buffer_write(buffer, buffer_u8, 1);
network_send_packet(socket, buffer, buffer_tell(buffer));
}
```

19. Place an instance each of `obj_client` and `obj_button` in the room.

Once these steps are complete, you are free to test your new server/client relationship. Run a test of `network_type_server.gmx` and, while it is still running, run a test of `network_type_client.gmx`. Press the button and see what happens!

How it works...

Alright, take a deep breath now. GameMaker's networking code may seem a little daunting, but it is much easier to understand once you know how to read it. Let's unpack the code in order to understand what is really going on here. Just a heads up; we're going to discuss several terms and coding methods that haven't been discussed in the previous chapters, but these methods can be used to facilitate the creation of new games in the future.

To start with, you'll notice that we're using two different project files in order to complete our task. The reason for this is that we're essentially creating two elements: the program or game (the client) and server. The server is a program that acts as the central hub for the overall game. Its purpose is to control the flow of data, collect information from a single or multiple sources (the clients), and store and/or distribute it to the appropriate connected client(s). This can happen in one of the two ways: a server-to-client connection or a client-to-client connection. In this recipe, we'll focus on a server-to-client connection.

Beginning with the **Create** event in the server program, we will initialize two elements: the server and socket. To simplify things, let's take a look at the definitions of each of them and their respective options:

> ▸ **Server**: Before we can even consider sending information across a network, we need to initialize the server. To do so, we use the `network_create_server` function (server type, port, and max clients). Let's break this down even further. The server type will be either `network_socket_TCP` or `network_socket_UDP`. The `network_socket_bluetooth` argument is technically packaged in GameMaker but is not *actually* supported, so don't waste your time there.
>
> The main difference between the **Transmission Control Protocol** (TCP) and **User Datagram Protocol** (**UDP**) is that the TCP is connection-oriented whereas the UDP is connectionless. What this means is that, while information sent via the TCP travels in a stream directly from one connection to another (such as information sent over the Internet), information sent via the UDP is sent via loads of packets all at once, after which the affiliation is deemed complete. The TCP is slower but the data sent is guaranteed to arrive in the order in which it was sent. The UDP, on the other hand, is much faster but the data is not even guaranteed to arrive at all. Because of its inherent speed, the UDP is much better suited for online games but, because we're sending small amounts of data guaranteed to be received in sequence, we're using TCP for this recipe. The port is a window through which data obtained is identified by a numerical value ranging from 0 (which means no port) to 65535.
>
> There are many well-known and reserved port numbers, a list of which can be found on Wikipedia, so it is best to use a higher number when you assign your port. For this reason, we're using a port number that is over 9000. The client will use the same port to connect to the server and begin sending and receiving data. Last (and the most straightforward) is the maximum number of clients allowed by the server. Here, we're setting this value to 8, which means a total of eight users can connect directly to the server. According to the documentation, this number tops at 1000 (a seemingly arbitrary number), but many users report issues with anything more than 64 simultaneous users. I recommend that you use a lower cap for maximum users as the more users on the server, the greater the memory strain. If, however, your game requires more users, this is still a possibility.

▶ **Socket**: A network socket is an endpoint of data that listens for connections via the assigned port. If the port is a window for receiving data, then the socket is someone standing at the said window, looking for the right data. When we created the server object, there was no one connected. Therefore, we assign the `noone` value to the `socket` variable. This value will change as soon as a client connects.

In the **Networking** event, we can see how the server handles client connections, disconnections, and incoming data. Before we try to understand how this is done, we first need to know a bit about data structures. Data structures are used to store and recall pieces of information in a precise fashion, such as in a certain order in a list or in a certain position on a grid. While you can use an array in the same fashion, calling and storing more complex information in this way will require large chunks of code that will use valuable system resources to unpack and execute. For this reason, YoYo Games added the use of six types of data structures to streamline the whole process: stacks, queues, lists, maps, priority queues, and grids. In our case, we'll require the use of data structure maps or `ds_maps`. One `ds_map` function in particular, `async_load`, is created in the **Networking** event automatically and cannot be used outside this event. The `async_load` is already populated with specific keys, which is all that we will require from it. Normally, when using `ds_maps`, you will need to initialize the `ds_map` function, populate it with the information (keys), and call or manipulate this information using specific functions. Since `async_load` is already initialized and contains our prerequisite data, we can refer to it without using all of the `ds_map` functions we would use otherwise. The `async_load` is called an accessor and works like a one-dimensional array in which there is only one set of keys. In `async_load`, we can call seven different keys, depending on which network event is taking place. The `type`, `id`, `ip`, and `port` keys are common to all network functions received during this event. If, however, the event is a connection or disconnection, you can access the `socket` key, which will hold the socket ID. If you are receiving data, you will have access to the `buffer` key, which contains the buffer ID, and the `size` key, which correlates to the size of the buffer data being received.

What we need at this point is for GameMaker to know what type of networking event will take place whenever this code is run. To do this, we need to access the `type` key in `async_load` by packing `async_load[? "type]` into the `typeEvent` variable. Here, we need to use a `switch` statement. A `switch` statement will check a specific value and then execute the code based on the results. This result can also be achieved by running several `if` statements, but a `switch` statement will do it with less code while using fewer resources. In our case, we check the value of the `type` key in `async_load`. If `type` is equal to `network_type_connect` (a client is connecting), then we check whether the value of `socket` is noone. If this is the case, then we assign the value of the `async_load` key `socket` to the `socket` variable after which the code is complete. If `type` is not a connection, we move on to check whether it is equal to `network_type_disconnect` (a disconnection). If *this* is the case, we assign the `socket` variable the value of `noone` and end the code. Otherwise, we move on to verify that the `type` is equal to `network_type_data`, which means that data has been sent. If the data is sent, we want GameMaker to take the value of the `async_load` key `buffer` and assign it to our `buffer` variable.

In order to access the information in the buffer (in order to read from it or write to it), we need to tell GameMaker to access it and from what point. For this, we use `buffer_seek`. The `buffer_seek` requires three arguments: the buffer you wish to access (we're accessing the buffer we stored in the `buffer` variable), the position at which you would like to begin the said access (we're using `buffer_seek_start` to start from the beginning), and the data offset value (you can use this to access more specific points by searching for an adjacent position x bytes away from your set starting point; we've chosen 0, so we are not using an offset value). The `switch` statement will run through this code until it finds a match. You'll notice that we're also using the `break` function. This is to ensure that GameMaker does not keep comparing the value of `type` after it has found a match. Using break is not necessary; you can leave it out and let the code run in its entirety without any issues in many cases. We're using it here because we're dealing with data being sent across a network and we want to save resources wherever we can.

Once we've accessed the beginning of the buffer and data is incoming from the client, the next line of code will allow GameMaker to run the `scr_packetReceive` script with our buffer being passed to the script. Scripts are very similar to the code blocks we use, as they are written using GML. The difference is that scripts work more like a function, taking the name you give the script in the script editor. Just like any other function in GML, your script will require arguments in order to be executed. These arguments are passed to the script itself, which is to be used in the code. For example, our script has one argument to which we assign the contents of the `buffer` variable. In the script code, this becomes `argument[0]`, as it is the first (and in this case only) argument we use. Once your code reaches the script, it will be run just like a standard function with the arguments you enter, providing the data necessary to execute.

 Scripts can be saved and loaded into GameMaker via `.txt` files, making scripts incredibly useful by allowing you to create prefab code blocks that can be used in future projects.

To understand this further, let's take a look at the script we created here. When a client sends data to the server, we run the script with our buffer, which is provided as `argument[0]`. In the script, we pass `argument[0]` (our buffer) to the `buffer` variable. Next, we take the `buffer_read` function (which should be self-explanatory) and pack it into the `message_id` variable. The `buffer_read` function requires two arguments of its own: the index of the buffer to read and the data type constant. The data type constant used here is `buffer_u8`, which is an unsigned, 8-bit integer that ranges from 0-255; in our case, it's 1. For our purposes, this simply tells the server that the button has been pressed (we'll take a look at why in a moment). The `message_id` is then used for another `switch` statement. However, for our recipe, we're only offering one outcome: if the information has been passed from the client (that is, the button has been pressed), then we need to execute this code. The code in question simply creates an instance of `obj_signal` in a random place on the screen under the server project. The only thing `obj_signal` does is draw the text **Hello, World**, wherever it is created, letting us know that we were successful in sending data across the network.

Taking a slight step back, the final thing we must do is destroy the server whenever the game ends. This is done to kill the connection, as an unchecked server connection left open is never a good thing. This also prevents memory leaks. To do so, we use `network_destroy(server)` to end this particular connection on the server side.

Now, let's create a client. As mentioned earlier, since we're trying to establish a connection between two programs, we need to create a separate program for the client. As with any Internet connection, our connection requires an IP address, specifically yours. For the purpose of learning how to create a network connection in GameMaker, we will store the address in the `ip` variable. There are different ways to find your IP address, including entering `What is my IP address?` in a Google search. One caveat is that you need to know the difference between a private network address and public address. Your private network address is the IP address of the particular device you are using, as it pertains to your network. When you connect to your router, your device is assigned an IP address that will likely resemble `192.168.xxx.xxx` in which `xxx` is a number between 0 and 255. Your public IP address is the number assigned to your Internet access point (such as your modem); it follows the same layout as a private address, but it is unique to your connection. When you store your IP address in the `ip` variable, you have two options: you can connect two devices to the same private network by entering your private IP address, or you can connect two devices to the Internet by entering your public IP address. Since you would need to connect to two separate access points to test the latter, I would recommend that you use your private IP address for the moment.

Next, we need to create a network socket using, you guessed it right, `network_create_socket(network type)`. This is where we establish the client's point of connection to the server. This is followed by creating the connection itself using `network_connect()`, in which we plug the socket, IP address, and port information in order to connect to the proper server. Once this is complete, we can use `buffer_create(size, type, and alignment)` to create the buffer that will send our data to the server. The arguments required to use this function are quite important as they determine how the buffer data is stored and accessed. The buffer's size is fairly straightforward. This is the size of the buffer itself in bytes. We've chosen 1024, which is quite small. Keep your buffer size in mind when you program network connections; use a large enough buffer that can store the data you need to transmit at once but not so large that it will slow down or crash the program. The buffer type can be of four different varieties: a `fixed` buffer, `grow` buffer, `wrap` buffer, and `fast` buffer. The `fixed` buffer, as the name implies, has a `fixed` buffer size, which remains constant. If there is more data than your buffer has room for, any remaining data will be lost. I prefer to use this type whenever possible, especially if there is little data being sent. The `grow` buffer will grow to accommodate additional data but comes at a cost: the buffer will grow until it reaches a capacity that can handle the amount of data you want to store, but it does so incrementally and copies its entire contents every time it does. This can prove to be a drain on the CPU and is likely to slow down your game. It is viable to use this type of buffer in your projects, but make sure you give it a healthy size to begin with.

A large buffer may use more memory, but the CPU drain to increase it should be a last resort. A `wrap` buffer is similar to a `grow` buffer in such a way that it can accommodate more incoming data, but it does this by looping to the start of the buffer and overwriting the information whenever the buffer's end is reached. I don't often recommend this buffer type as you have no control over what data is overwritten. The last type of buffer is the `fast` buffer, which can only accommodate 8-bit integers, signed or unsigned, and nothing more. Finally, the buffer's alignment tells GameMaker to write data in intervals. An alignment of 1 byte ensures that every piece of data will remain sequential, with no gaps. An alignment of 2 bytes, however, will assign a space in groups of two. This means that a 1-byte chunk of data will take up two data spaces, with the second one being empty. A 4-byte chunk of data will fit in the parameters, which means that it will take up two sets of two data spaces with no empty spaces between them and the next chunk of data. You can get by mostly using an alignment of 1 byte, but it can prove to be faster to use a larger alignment if some data is sent in larger chunks. A useful analogy I once heard is, "It's easier to read separate words than a block of text with no spaces." We've created our buffer; now, it's time to use it.

The client's create event sets up the connection at this end, but the button object is where the action is. This is where we tell GameMaker to take some data, hand it to the buffer, and pass it to the server to take action. The data we're sending in this example is minimal, mind you, but it demonstrates exactly how a network-to-server connection works. Given that the connection is made through the client object, we first need to tell GameMaker that we're executing the code using the client object, even though the button object is the one being clicked. For this, we need to use a `with()` construction. As we've seen in the previous chapters, a `with` construction simply executes the given code as if it is executed by the client object itself. Now that this has been established, we need to find the beginning of the buffer, with no offset, using `buffer_seek` and then begin writing to it using `buffer_write(buffer, type, value)`. Here, we must tell GameMaker which buffer we wish to use (the one we packed into the `buffer` variable), what type of data we're entering (an unsigned 8-bit integer between 0 and 255), and the actual contents of that data (in our case, the value is 1). We're writing to the buffer only once, but you can write several pieces of data using `buffer_write` multiple times. Since we're using a TCP connection, however, you need to keep in mind that the order in which the data is written to the buffer is the same order in which it will be read at the other end. We're now ready to send our data to the server. For this, we're using `network_send_packet(the socket, buffer, and size)`. The socket and buffer are already packed into their respective variables, so that part is easy to read, but the buffer size is a little convoluted. When we created the buffer, we set its size to 1024. This was the maximum size, the largest amount of data we could pack at once. When we send the data to the server, it's not so much interested in this information as it is in knowing how much data is *currently* packed into the buffer. What `buffer_tell` does is provides the seek position of the end of the data. When you're driving your car, you don't want to know how much gas your tank can hold, you want to know how much is in it. The `buffer_tell` is your gas gauge.

In our example, `buffer_tell` will return a value of 1, since we're only sending one byte of data. Now, if you set the alignment to a higher value, say 4, and pack 1-byte of data, `buffer_tell` will still return 1. If you're sending two pieces of data, 1-byte and 4-bytes, `buffer_tell` will return 8 because it takes the spaces left by the alignment when returning the seek position.

Assuming that you entered your private network IP address in the `ip` variable, you can actually test this recipe on one machine. Simply, open both the projects at once, run the server, and then run the client. Once the client is connected, the **Compile** tab at the bottom of the screen on the server project will show that the client is connected successfully. Once the connection is established, clicking on the button on the client object will pack data (in this case, a value of 1) into the buffer and send it to the server. The server will see that a network event has taken place and, on recognizing that the data has been sent, it will run the script. The script will take the data (again, a value of 1) and, because the data has been sent, it will create an instance of `obj_signal` in a random place on the screen in the compiled server project, demonstrating that the connection remains successful. As I mentioned earlier, you can pack multiple pieces of data into the buffer to be sent at once. If you do this, the script will read all of it and act accordingly every time you press the button.

In a very large nutshell, this is how GameMaker handles a simple client-to-server connection.

Setting up asynchronous play for a turn-based game

I have a confession to make: Some of my favorite games are turn-based. That's right, I said it. I love games such as *XCOM* and *Heroes of Might and Magic*. When I was 13, I would unknowingly spend my entire day playing Sid Meier's *Civilization II*. I would go to the computer room (where there were no windows) in the morning and not come out until dark. I would mostly play against the game's AI but with faster Internet speeds and a greater focus on social gaming, I can enjoy these games with anyone, anywhere. Let's take a look at how to create a 2 two-player turn-based minesweeper game using GameMaker.

Getting ready

This recipe requires only one project file, though you'll need to run it twice in order to test it. Before we begin, you'll need a few objects: `obj_tileRed` and `obj_tileBlue` (each with their respective sprites and origins set to 0,0), `obj_connection`, `obj_game`, and `obj_tileParent`. You will also need a 768 x 768 room.

How to do it...

1. In each of `obj_tileRed` and `obj_tileBlue`, set the parent to `obj_tileParent`.

2. In `obj_tileParent`, add a **Create** event.

3. Drag a code block to the **Actions** box and add the following code:

```
isBomb = false;
```

4. Add a **Left Mouse Button Pressed** event to a code block.

5. Enter the following code:

```
if myTurn = true
{
    if !isBomb
    {
        buffer = buffer_create(1024, buffer_fixed, 1);
        buffer_seek(buffer, buffer_seek_start, 0);
        buffer_write(buffer, buffer_u8, 1);
        receiver = noone;
        if currentServer = true
        {
            receiver = obj_connection.client;
        }
        else
        {
            receiver = obj_connection.socket;
        }
        network_send_packet(receiver, buffer, buffer_
tell(buffer));
        buffer_delete(buffer);
        myTurn = false;
        instance_destroy();
    }
    else
    {
        game_end()
    }
}
```

6. In `obj_game`, add a **Create** event and drag a code block to the **Actions** box.

7. Enter the following code:

```
var i, j;
for (i=0; i<12; i++)
    for (j=0; j<12; j++)
```

```
        {
            if ((i mod 2==0 && j mod 2==0)||(i mod 2==1 && j mod
    2==1))
            {
                instance_create(64*i, 64*j, obj_tileRed);
            }
            else
            {
                instance_create(64*i, 64*j, obj_tileBlue);
            }
        }
    scr_dropBombs(10);
```

8. In `obj_connection`, add a **Create** event.

9. Place a code block in the **Actions** box and enter the following code:

```
    globalvar currentServer;
    globalvar myTurn;
    globalvar player_id;
    networkType = network_socket_tcp;
    ip = "xxx.xxx.x.xxx"; //Replace with your own IP address

    socket = network_create_socket(networkType);
    connection = network_connect(socket, ip, 9001);
    currentServer = false;
    player_id = "Player 2";
    myTurn = false;

    if (connection < 0)
    {
    player_id = "Player 1";
    myTurn = true;
    server = network_create_server(networkType, 9001, 1);
    network_destroy(socket);
    currentServer = true;
    client = noone;
    }
```

10. Add a **Networking** event.

11. Place a code block in the **Actions** box and enter the following code:

```
    typeEvent = async_load[? "type"];
    switch(typeEvent)
    {
```

```
case network_type_connect:
if(!currentServer)
break;
if (client == noone)
{
client = async_load[? "socket"];
}
break;

case network_type_disconnect:
if (!currentServer) break;
client = noone;
break;

case network_type_data:
var buffer = async_load[? "buffer"];
buffer_seek(buffer, buffer_seek_start, 0);
scr_packetReceive(buffer);
break;
}
```

12. Add a **Draw** event to a code block.

13. Enter the following code:

```
draw_text(2, 0, player_id);
if myTurn = true
{
    draw_text(room_width/2, 0, "Go!");
}
else
{
    draw_text(room_width/2, 0, "Please wait.");
}
```

14. Add a **Game End** event and drag a code block to the **Actions** box.

15. Enter the following code:

```
if (currentServer)
{
    network_destroy(server);
}
else
{
    network_destroy(socket);
}
```

16. Create a script called `scr_packetReceive` and enter the following code:

```
buffer = argument[0];
message_id  = buffer_read(buffer, buffer_u8);
myTurn = true;
```

17. Create a second script called `scr_dropBombs` and enter the following code:

```
var bombs, bombMax;
bombMax = argument[0];

bombs = ds_list_create();
ds_list_clear(bombs);
with(obj_tileParent)
{
    ds_list_add(bombs, id);
}
ds_list_shuffle(bombs);

for (i=0; i<bombMax; i++)
{
    with(ds_list_find_value(bombs, i))
    {
        isBomb = true;
    }
}
ds_list_destroy(bombs);
```

18. Place one instance each of `obj_connection` and `obj_game` in the room.

Once this is complete, you are ready to test it. Open two instances of the project and run one of them. Once the game is active (and the board has been generated), run the second one and you're ready to go.

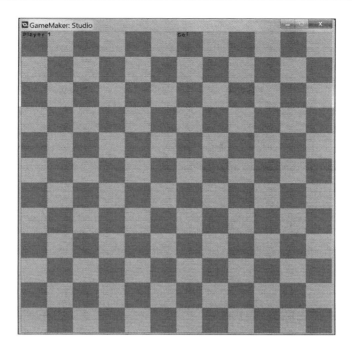

How it works...

This recipe works in a similar manner to the previous recipe with one major difference: instead of having a dedicated server, each of the client programs takes turns to act as the server for the other. Let's take a look at how this can be accomplished. Many aspects of this recipe are straightforward or have been discussed in the previous chapters, so we'll stick to the heavier stuff.

Let's begin with the board itself. First, we need to lay out our tiles in a checkerboard pattern. To accomplish this, we use nested `for` loops to establish the origin points for each object in our grid (the objects being `obj_tileRed` and `obj_tileBlue`). We set the room to 768 x 768 so that we can run these loops until both i and j equal 12. During these loops, GameMaker will check for instances in which i mod 2 and j mod 2 are equal to 0, or i mod 2 and j mod 2 are equal to 1. In these cases, GameMaker will create an instance of `obj_tileRed` in which the *x* and *y* coordinates are i and j times 64, respectively. Otherwise, GameMaker will create an instance of `obj_tilBlue` using the same equation for the coordinates. This creates a pattern that alternates between the two objects, thus creating a checkerboard effect. After this, we run our `scr_dropBombs` script in order to place bombs in random places, corresponding to this grid, with the argument acting as the maximum number of bombs to be placed (10, in our case).

If you take a look at the bomb script, you can see that we are creating a data structure list that is similar to the one that we discussed in *Chapter 9, Particle Man, Particle Man – Adding Polish to Your Game with Visual Effects and Particles*. Here, we must initiate, populate, and access data in this `ds_list`. First, we use `ds_list_create` to initialize the list and `ds_list_clear` to ensure that it is empty. We use a `With` construction in conjunction with `obj_tileParent` (which is connected to each of the tiles) and we add the object ID to each position in the list. The ID is the identification number assigned to every object in the room, which is based on the order in which it was created. Once this is complete, we use `ds_list_shuffle` to randomize the list of IDs and use a `for` loop to take the first 10 and turn them into bombs by making `isBomb` true. When we're done with this, we use `ds_list_destroy` to destroy the list and move on.

Next, we'll set up the most important part of our multiplayer experience: the connection. In the **Create** event of our connection object, you will see some familiar functions. As mentioned earlier, we must create our connection, but things are a little different this time. We want GameMaker to create a client connection and search for a server. If a server is found, the `currentServer` variable becomes `false` (for obvious reasons), the `player_id` variable becomes **Player 2** (making you **Player 2**), and `myTurn` becomes `false` (which means **Player 1**, the server, goes first). Now, if there is no server running when this takes place, GameMaker will return a value of less than 0. If this happens, we make some changes. The `player_id` variable becomes **Player 1**, `myTurn` becomes `true`, we create a server and destroy the socket (client), `currentServer` becomes `true`, and the client becomes `noone` because there is no client connected as yet. All of this is going to happen when you run the first instance of the project for testing. Because of this, the first one will take a little longer to fully run, and you'll see the socket timeout before it stops trying to connect as a client and starts as a server.

The next most important thing to know is what's going on in the **Networking** event. This code is very similar to the code found in the server project of the previous recipe. This is where we use `async_load ds_map` and a `switch` event to determine what type of a network event we're working with at the moment and how it should be handled. Did you notice what's different? Because the role of the server alternates between what is essentially the two instances of the same program, when connecting or disconnecting, we need to check whether we're currently playing the server or not. If we're currently playing the server, we hit a break. We don't, however, need to do this if the network event is the incoming data. If this is the case, we know for sure that we're playing the server. If the data is incoming, we need to run our `Packet Receive` script, but before we check this out, let's take a look at what happens when we make our move in the game.

If we take a look at the **Left Mouse Button Pressed** event in `obj_tileParent`, we can see where our buffer is created. First things first, though, GameMaker needs to know if it's our turn. If it's not our turn, then none of the next code is compiled. Assuming that it is, we need to send some data through the buffer to the server. Once again, we will use a fixed buffer with a 1024 byte size. There is more than enough room to send the data required. Here, we're only packing one piece of data into the buffer: the number 1, which will act as our argument. Since this information is in the form of an integer between 0 and 255, we can use `buffer_u8` to send it to the other side. Once we've done this, we must then determine the data's recipient. Since we would normally send this from the client to the server via the socket and as there is no permanent server, we need to establish who the receiver is using an `if/else` statement. We first set the receiver variable to `noone` and then set our stipulations. If we're the current server, the receiver becomes `obj_connection.client` otherwise, it becomes `obj_connection.socket`. Once this has been established, we can use `network_send_packet` to send our data through. Next, we must delete the buffer, remove our turn (set `myTurn` to `false`), and then destroy the tile that was clicked in the first place. Now, all of this takes place *only if the tile is not a bomb*. If it *is* a bomb, GameMaker ignores all of the code and simply ends the game because the bomb went off.

Once the data is sent to the acting server, the server must then read the data and act upon it. In this case, we only tell GameMaker that a network event has taken place, at which point we set `myTurn` to `true` and start the process all over again.

There's more...

When testing this recipe, you may be curious to know whether the bombs are populating properly or not, or where they are. One concern could be whether the bombs are populating in the same tiles from client-to-client or not. In order to put your mind at ease, you need to perform the following steps:

1. Create a 64 x 64 sprite of a black circle called `spr_bomb`.
2. Add a **Draw** event to `obj_game`.
3. Drop a code block in the **Actions** box and add the following code:

```
with(obj_tileParent)
{
    if isBomb = true
    {
        draw_sprite(spr_bomb, -1, x, y);
    }
}
```

This will draw the bomb sprite on top of any tile in which `isBomb` is `true`, which means that the tile is a bomb. Go ahead and test it out!

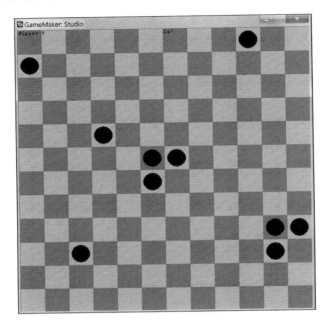

Index

Symbols

2D movement
  creating 25-27
3D audio 84

A

analogue joystick acceleration
  utilizing 37, 38
asynchronous play
  setting up, for turn-based game 180-187
audio basics 84

B

background data 120
background music
  importing 84-88
  playing 84-88
basic enemies
  programming 14-17
break function 177

C

character
  controlling, with keyboard 60-63
  controlling, with mouse 60-63
  making jump 28-30
  moving, by tilting device 42, 43
  moving, on grid 50, 51
clamp() function 149
client
  connecting, to server 172-179

collision options
  angular damping 73
  collision group 73
  density 72
  friction 73
  linear damping 73
  restitution 73
controller
  setting up 35, 36
controls
  gamepad controls 25
  keyboard controls 24
  mouse controls 24
  tilt controls 25
  touch controls 25
cursor
  following 33, 34

D

day/night cycle
  creating 142-144
Doppler effect
  replicating, with emitters 94-96
draw_text() function 131

E

enemy pathfinding
  creating 56-59
explosions
  creating 159-164

O

objects
  dragging, on grid 48, 49
  lighting, with spot light 139-141
  moving, by tilting device 42, 43
objects, that use physics
  creating 67-72
online play 172
onscreen objects
  dragging 47, 48

P

particles
  about 152
  URL 165
  used, to simulate kicking up dust 152-154
paths
  setting 52-56
  using 46
pause screen
  creating 125, 126
physics engine 101 66
player
  moving 5-7
player health
  setting up 17-19
player lives
  setting up 17-19
player selection
  saving 127-131
point-and-click interface
  using 31, 32
point_direction function 63, 64
projectiles
  adding 8-11

R

rainfall effect
  simulating 156-158
room, with light switch
  creating 137-139
rope
  creating 78-81
Run button
  adding 27, 28

S

save data
  decrypting 132-134
  encrypting 132-134
save systems 120
score
  saving 127-132
scoring mechanism
  creating 19, 20
screen-shake effect
  adding 165-167
server
  about 175
  client, connecting to 172-180
situational sound effects
  implementing 88-91
slow motion effect
  using 168, 169
sound effects 84
sound emitters
  adding 91, 92
splash pages
  creating 113-115
spot light
  used, for lighting objects 139-141
sprite
  animating 2-5
Super Mario World game 136
Super Smash Bros game 171
swipes
  using 40-42

T

tap control
  adding 38, 39
tilt controls 25
title screen
  adding 110-113
touch controls 25
Transmission Control Protocol (TCP) 175
turn-based game
  asynchronous play, setting up 180-187

U

User Datagram Protocol (UDP) 175

W

win/lose scenarios
  creating 21, 22

Y

YoYo Games
  URL 141

Thank you for buying
GameMaker Cookbook

About Packt Publishing

Packt, pronounced 'packed', published its first book, *Mastering phpMyAdmin for Effective MySQL Management*, in April 2004, and subsequently continued to specialize in publishing highly focused books on specific technologies and solutions.

Our books and publications share the experiences of your fellow IT professionals in adapting and customizing today's systems, applications, and frameworks. Our solution-based books give you the knowledge and power to customize the software and technologies you're using to get the job done. Packt books are more specific and less general than the IT books you have seen in the past. Our unique business model allows us to bring you more focused information, giving you more of what you need to know, and less of what you don't.

Packt is a modern yet unique publishing company that focuses on producing quality, cutting-edge books for communities of developers, administrators, and newbies alike. For more information, please visit our website at www.packtpub.com.

About Packt Open Source

In 2010, Packt launched two new brands, Packt Open Source and Packt Enterprise, in order to continue its focus on specialization. This book is part of the Packt open source brand, home to books published on software built around open source licenses, and offering information to anybody from advanced developers to budding web designers. The Open Source brand also runs Packt's open source Royalty Scheme, by which Packt gives a royalty to each open source project about whose software a book is sold.

Writing for Packt

We welcome all inquiries from people who are interested in authoring. Book proposals should be sent to author@packtpub.com. If your book idea is still at an early stage and you would like to discuss it first before writing a formal book proposal, then please contact us; one of our commissioning editors will get in touch with you.

We're not just looking for published authors; if you have strong technical skills but no writing experience, our experienced editors can help you develop a writing career, or simply get some additional reward for your expertise.

GameMaker Game Programming with GML

ISBN: 978-1-78355-944-2   Paperback: 350 pages

Learn GameMaker Language programming concepts and script integration with GameMaker: Studio through hands-on, playable examples

1. Write and utilize scripts to help organize and speed up your game production workflow.

2. Display important user interface components such as score, health, and lives.

3. Play sound effects and music, and create particle effects to add some spice to your projects.

4. Build your own example match-three puzzle and platform games.

GameMaker Essentials

ISBN: 978-1-78439-612-1   Paperback: 154 pages

Learn all the essential skills of GameMaker: Studio and start making your own impressive games with ease.

1. Learn the core aspects of GameMaker: Studio to create stunning games and share them with the world.

2. Learn how to create games in GameMaker using the GameMaker Language (GML).

3. A fast-paced, step-by-step guide that focuses on providing practical skills to develop applications.

Please check **www.PacktPub.com** for information on our titles

PUBLISHING

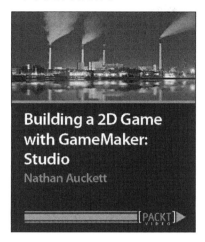

Building a 2D Game with GameMaker: Studio [Video]

ISBN: 978-1-78355-876-6   Duration: 2:13 hours

All you need to know to get started with GameMaker: Studio.

1. Learn how to use GameMaker: Studio and its interface.

2. Program in Game Maker Language (GML).

3. Create your very own artificial intelligence.

HTML5 Game Development with GameMaker

ISBN: 978-1-84969-410-0   Paperback: 364 pages

Experience a captivating journey that will take you from creating a full-on shoot 'em up to your first social web browser game

1. Build browser-based games and share them with the world.

2. Master the GameMaker Language with easy to follow examples.

3. Every game comes with original art and audio, including additional assets to build upon each lesson.

Please check **www.PacktPub.com** for information on our titles

Made in the USA
San Bernardino, CA
23 February 2016